SOCIOI ....

The Ultimate Guide to Sociopathy, Psychopathy, and Narcissism

(Expose the Sociopath Wreaking Havoc in Your Life)

Fairy Riggs

Published by Martin Debroh

Fairy Riggs

All Rights Reserved

Sociopath: The Ultimate Guide to Sociopathy, Psychopathy, and Narcissism (Expose the Sociopath Wreaking Havoc in Your Life)

ISBN 978-1-77485-108-1

Legal & Disclaimer

The information contained in this book is not designed to replace or take the place of any form of medicine or professional medical advice. The information in this book has been provided for educational and entertainment purposes only.

The information contained in this book has been compiled from sources deemed reliable, and it is accurate to the best of the Author's knowledge; however, the Author cannot guarantee its accuracy and validity and cannot be held liable for any errors or omissions. Changes are periodically made to this book. You must consult your doctor or get professional medical advice before using any of the suggested remedies, techniques, or information in this book.

Upon using the information contained in this book, you agree to hold harmless the Author from and against any damages, costs, and expenses, including any legal fees potentially resulting from the application of any of the information provided by this guide. This disclaimer applies to any damages or injury caused by the use and application, whether directly or indirectly, of any advice or information presented, whether for breach of contract, tort, negligence, personal injury, criminal intent, or under any other cause of action.

You agree to accept all risks of using the information presented inside this book. You need to consult a professional medical practitioner in order to ensure you are both able and healthy enough to participate in this program.

Table of Contents

Introduction

The term sociopathy and psychopathy are often used to describe the same disorder. However, there are many people who believe that, whilst the two disorders have very similar characteristics, there also some key differences. In fact the American Psychiatric Association acknowledges both disorders and lists them both under the heading of Antisocial Personality Disorders (ASPD). This book aims to discover the origins of the sociopath and the psychopath and what a sociopath actually is. The book will look at the characteristics of a sociopath, how to spot one and how to deal with one. It will also offer guidance on how to live either with a sociopath or how to live daily as a sociopath. Finally, the book will cover the treatment options available to sociopath's and the prospects for their future. As with many personality disorders; the support of family and friends can make a huge difference.

In a nutshell a sociopath is someone who will always look after themselves before anyone else and regardless of the effect their decisions have on other people. Their behaviour may be morally and ethically wrong but they will show no remorse for anything they do. In fact, sociopaths will often exploit other people for their own benefit; acting in a predatory way to ensure the outcome is the one they want.

It is believed that the sociopath finds it impossible to connect on an emotional level to any other person; this combines with a love of themselves to make it impossible to feel any kind of concern for their actions. It is this lack of awareness of other people and their effect on other people that allows a sociopath to be ruthless in the pursuit of their goals. The inability to connect with others removes many of the obstacles that most people encounter when trying to be successful in any walk of life. It is also this quality that makes it so difficult for anyone to understand the nature and intent of a sociopath.

A true sociopath does not necessarily have malicious intentions; in fact they can often be unaware of the real reasons why friends can no longer stand to be associated with them. A sociopath has very little emotional connection to anything else in life; this means they will treat other people as objects instead of people. The result of this is usually emotional hurt which can feel malicious but is not necessarily intended to be so. The key to this response is the fact that anyone who is not a sociopath will have the normal range of human emotions; this makes them vulnerable to the actions of a sociopath. The normal range of emotions requires you to think about any course of action and its consequences for both yourself and for anyone who else who could be affected by your actions. A sociopath is not limited by these feelings and is, therefore, able to act in any way they see fit.

Many sociopaths have such a complete love of themselves that they develop a belief that they are entitled to anything they want. This may seem outstanding to the average person, but, it is simply an extension of the lack of thought about others; the usual reasons as to why it is not possible to have everything you want simply do not apply to a sociopath.

Of course, there are different levels of sociopathy, just as there are different levels of any human personality traits. Some sociopaths are focused on what they desire and are simply aiming for that regardless of any emotional damage caused along the way. Others either are aware or become aware of the effect their actions can have on others. This allows them to manipulate and use others to achieve their own aims. These types of sociopaths are the most dangerous; they are able to present a normal image to society and will spend time perfecting this image. Underneath this respectable exterior they will be coolly calculating the best route to achieve their aims; including who and what can be used to assist them along the way.

The sociopath was first used in the late 1920's in an attempt to distinguish it from psychopathy; the differences between these will be discussed in much more detail in the first chapter. The main reason for this distinction was that medical professionals believed that any person or even a group of people could be shown to have the same tendencies as a sociopath; although these tend to be for limited periods in conjunction with a specific alm.

In these cases people are aware of the emotional damage to other people which can be caused but choose to ignore it for what they see as the greater good. This behaviour is the same as a sociopath but temporary. The sociopath only ever sees the greater good as their own goals, and always puts them first. In contrast it is not possible to be a psychopath for a temporary period.

The diagnosis and understanding of the sociopath has been investigated and adjusted many times over the second half of the twentieth century. It remains entwined with the concept of a psychopath; the reality is that many people with this disorder will ultimately turn to crime as they lack the moral compass to understand that their actions are wrong. If confronted with the effects of the behaviour they can quickly become angry, as they are unable to see what they have done is wrong. People with this disorder do not dwell on the past or think excessively about the future; they live in the now and in many ways are isolated from those around them even though they may appear to be the life of the party.

Diagnosing someone as a sociopath is not easy; the majority of people do not see what they are doing as wrong so cannot see an issue with the way they behave. If you do not perceive yourself as ill then you will not seek help! The best way to tell if someone is a sociopath is for a medical professional to ask them a series of questions; their responses and behaviour must be consistent. Although it is not yet clear whether a sociopath is made by nature or nurture, the traits of a sociopath must be displayed during late childhood; these will develop in adulthood and can be influenced, to some extent, by the environment around them.

Chapter 1: What Is Sociopathy?

Sociopathy is a particular term which is used to describe a group of personality traits which primarily include a disregard for the rights of other people, inability to conform to the customs of society, inability to form emotional and personal relationships, a lack of remorse or empathy towards other people, and a frequent manipulation and deception of others.

The term sociopathy is often used interchangeably with the terms psychopathy and antisocial personality disorder. However, while all these three terms may all basically refer to a similar particular mental condition, the main distinction lies in the establishment of a formal diagnosis.

Under the Diagnostic and Statistical Manual of Mental Disorders, 5th Edition (DSM-5) of the American Psychiatric Association, a sociopathic or psychopathic individual is formally medically diagnosed as a person suffering from antisocial personality disorder – a certain type of personality disorder which is especially characterized with a long-standing pattern of behaviors that includes the manipulation, exploitation, or even the violation of the rights, feelings, or safety of others without remorse.

On the other hand, between sociopathy and psychopathy, the main difference lies on the origin of the condition. While psychopathy is considered to be of biological cause or origin, sociopathy is considered to be caused by a combination of genetic factors and environmental influences. Hence, psychopaths are basically born while sociopathic individuals are made. Psychopathy is also considered to be a much more severe form of sociopathy.

General Manifestation of Sociopathy

Sociopathy is primarily characterized with impairments in the conscience of a person. A sociopath does not have one, has a conscience full of holes, or has the ability to entirely negate or neutralize any perception or sense of conscience. This allows them to do immoral acts without even having troubled thoughts or a disturbed sleep afterwards.

Sociopathic individuals or those diagnosed with antisocial personality disorder may often be associated with criminal behaviors, may habitually engage in acts which dangerously skirt the boundaries of the law, or may hurt other people in ways which may not particularly be considered criminal, but enough to be considered as highly immoral and unethical.

While it is typically normal to automatically associate the word 'criminal' with the word 'sociopath', it is important to take note of the fact that not all sociopaths go around society wreaking obvious havoc, such as serious crimes and other acts which are totally against the law.

It is essential to be aware of the very important fact that some sociopaths are able to successfully blend in with other people in the society and are only causing damages to others in the form of emotional and psychological devastation, acts which may not be typically punishable by law. Sociopaths are not just the serial killers or the evident lawbreakers of society. They could be your neighbor, your friend, your partner, your family member, or your boss.

High functioning sociopaths, for instance, is a particular term which pertains to individuals with sociopathic traits who also happen to have exceptionally high levels of intelligent quotient (IQ) which then gives them the ability plan in a very meticulous manner. These individuals are typically very successful in their chosen field of interest and may make it hard for other individuals to compete with them due to their lack of empathy and remorse and their extreme capabilities to manipulate and deceive.

As to the prevalence of sociopathy or antisocial personality disorder, it has been found that 1 out of every 25 people suffer from this condition. And considering the fact that the individuals exhibiting sociopathic traits may pose certain levels of danger to the people they encounter or constantly mingle with, there is indeed a great need for an accurate diagnosis and the consequent application of the best treatment option.

Chapter 2: Manipulative Behavior

One of the main characteristics of a sociopath is his ability to manipulate others. A sociopath is a master manipulator and actually takes pride over his manipulations. This manipulator doesn't discriminate who he manipulates, they will manipulate and lie to anyone they cross paths with. These people may be someone they just met at the grocery store, it may be their teacher, it may even be their parent. It doesn't matter who it is, a sociopath will do everything in his power to try and manipulate them. Before a manipulator can manipulate you or a situation, the often become very familiar with who you are. Sociopaths are able to read people quite easily. They are able to single out victims who are more trusting and easily influenced over others. These individuals are people watchers, they are individuals who can not only read people but they are able to study them and figure them out in a very short amount of time. Sociopaths often stalk others in order to find out details about them, their habits and what they like and what they don't like. When they are able to identify someone weak and vulnerable these vulnerable individuals become prey for these predators. Finding individuals who are weak is easy for sociopaths. They will often find individuals whose insecurities are obvious and in plain view. They may find someone who seems shy, or someone who's quite, they may even find someone whose physical appearance may be different than others. When someone has insecurities, it's often quite obvious to others, especially to sociopaths who pride themselves on reading people. If someone is a weak individual, they are often easily influences by others, especially someone who is charming, someone who may even convince them that they can fix whatever is wrong in their lives. That being said, the sociopath takes advantage of those who are weak and who may be looking for a leader in their life.

When relationships start with a sociopath, it's because the victim is manipulated into the friendship and relationship with the sociopath. When we're manipulated, we tend to not only believe everything that someone says, but we also start to feel as though we need this person in our life. That need can be incredibly overwhelming. When we feel as though we need someone, this is when the relationship becomes unhealthy. Overtime, this need is taken advantage of because the sociopath realizes how the victim feels. If the sociopath threatens to take themselves out of the victim's life, the victim will often do anything to prevent this from happening because they are under the sociopath's control. When we are manipulated by someone, the relationship becomes one sided with the sociopath having full control over the situation. This is also a sign to watch for in relationships. If you find that your significant other is manipulating you and threatening to leave unless you do certain things, take a deeper look into the situation and make sure they are not showing other signs of sociopathic behavior. A sociopath is definitely not someone you want to date. Not only is this type of relationship unhealthy but it's also incredibly dangerous!

A sociopath has an agenda, they know what they want and that's to manipulate others and get them to complete tasks for them just for the fun of it. This agenda is often completed by those who fall under their spell and believe everything they say. Manipulation can be done in many different ways. Children can often manipulate other children into doing things for them by convincing them that it's the right thing to do. Maybe a child will tell another child who they see as weak that they'll be their friend if they steal for them or hurt someone else for them. A recent case where two children were involved in an attempted murder against one of their friends showed manipulative behavior and showed possible signs of sociopathic behavior as well. One friend convinced her other friend to help murder their friend by telling her that if she didn't help kill her, a fictional character would kill her entire family. With this specific case, one girl convinced her friend to try and kill their other friend by having her believe that her family would be killed if she didn't follow what she said. There are many cases like this where one person leads a disturbing act by getting others to either help them commit a crime or having others do it for them. Manipulation can also be done by making others either feel guilty or by making others feel needed. For example, maybe a sociopath convinces someone to do something for them by telling them they'll go on a date with them or they'll do something else to help them. Keep in mind that these master manipulators often prey on shy, insecure individuals who are in need of love and affection, no matter who it comes from.

For example, many individuals who are involved in sex trafficking are often sociopaths. They convince young, insecure girls to join them and promise to give them a better life. These girls are often persuaded by these sociopaths because they are so charming and convincing. The fact that they are able to manipulate these girls into having sexual intercourse for money shows you how manipulative these individuals can be. Along with the manipulation, these sociopaths who convince girls to become involved in this type of life do not feel any empathy or remorse for their actions. They do not feel as though they are doing anything wrong even though they are selling these young, innocent girls for sex, feeding these girls drugs and encouraging them to live an incredibly dangerous life. This reason alone, shows their lack of empathy, their lack of remorse and it shows that they do not care or have any feeling regarding their negative actions. These individuals simply want others to do what they say and when they do, they receive a great deal of satisfaction from this.

Chapter 3: Is This How It's Supposed To Be?

Let's talk about disrespectful behaviour.

Everybody Can Shout in Anger

Am I right?

Say you had a day from hell, that had been preceeded by weeks or months of frustration for whatever stressful situation that you are going through, then you get back home and without even realising it you are engaging on a huge fight with your partner over something so stupid that you find yourself saying 'It's not what you did, is how you did it!!!'. And that's being human. You get a build up of repressed anger and frustration and one day you simply burst and let it all out in one go, unfortunately directed to your partner because they dropped the last drop that tipped you over.

And like opening Pandora's box, you are letting all the demons come out, damaging the person that is closer to you in the process, the very person that is supposed to be the one that always takes your side and supports you.

It is not nice. Not to you and not to your other half. And if there are children in the house, it will definitely be scary for them too. Unless they are used to it.

You see the difference there? I will point it out: Unless they are used to it. That is when you need to have a hard look at what is happening at home, because it's happening all too often.

And if your children don't react anymore to your arguments, it's happening unreasonably often. This is abusive behaviour.

You are allowed to be human, and to have limits. That's just normal.

What isn't normal is when this happens every other day. Or when you actively come home to shout at your partner to vent your daily frustrations. Or vice versa, your partner doing it to you, and you being the doormat. Don't forget here that the person that chooses to stay with you is the person that chooses to support you and take your side. If that isn't happening, or if you are repeatedly damaging the only person that is there for you, you need to know that it isn't right.

Let's make a point here:

Continuous arguments **against** your other half is not normal.

Out of the Heat of the Argument

How about name calling, belittling, demeaning, non-constructive criticism, lying or hiding truths, setting you up to fail, and contradicting and opposing you by rule rather than reason?

Any of those disrespectful traits can be done in the heat of an argument, but it is when they are used regularly when our warning bells should be ringing the louder.

For instance, in a heated argument you could enter a state of rage that you might not be able to control, and you might insult your partner. It's not good, it's not pretty, **it shouldn't happen**, and if it did **you should regret it straight away**, and make a point of not doing it again because **it's hurtful and wrong to attack the person that loves you**.

If you both understand that, it won't happen often. If it does happen often, there is a problem.

Another one to watch out: Say that you have some sort of small defect, something physical about you that you might be self conscious about, like your eyes aren't exactly straight, or your size is on the generous side of the scale, or your laugh is too high pitch, and your partner makes an "innocent" jape pointing it out.

Just to be sure that we are on the same page, we are talking here about mocking, and not fond comments. Still, say it only happened once, hence no biggie so far.

Say that you are comfortably sitting on the sofa watching a show with your partner, and something happens that makes him or her jokingly mention your little "defect" again, and you both laugh about it. So far it's innocent: Everybody laughs at their own defects, right?

But do they? Or is it only about **your** defect? In other words: Are you the only one being mocked?

And does it get mentioned often? Did your partner give you a nickname for it? Are you now Fatty, or Hyena, and are jokes about having an eye in Boston and another one in California a recurrent thing?

First of all this shouldn't happen. Your partner shouldn't give you nicknames over things that you feel conscious about.

Secondly, this definitely shouldn't happen as a recurrent joke. If it made you feel bad already, your partner shouldn't laugh about it again.

Thirdly, if you have to explain to your partner that he or she **should not hurt your feelings for fun**, maybe you are just too different.

Respect for your feelings is a must have. Don't miss it out.

When it Becomes Bullying

Typically, if asking your partner to stop recurrent (hurtful) mocking because it's unfair and it makes you feel bad, you get either one of these answers:

C'mon it was just a joke.

OK, OK, I won't do it again.

But in both cases it happens again about the same defect or another one, it is not OK.

Your partner shouldn't need to disrespect you to get a laugh.

Hurting your partner's feelings out of an ongoing dispute is wrong, but it could happen in the heat of the moment and that's life. However, you should not feel good about doing it, and there should be an element of regret.

When there isn't, you are bullying the other person: Bullies don't care about hurting feelings, they think it's a joke.

That is why they won't feel bad for calling you fatty or mocking you in any other harmful way. They won't regret it and they won't see that they are doing something wrong because to them it's not that big a deal, and perceive it as actually quite funny.

But however bullies feel about what they are doing, the reality is that while you are in a relationship with this person your feelings do count, and **that behaviour is unacceptable whether they understand it or not**. No difference.

The good news is that you don't have to put up with it, and that it is completely up to you to set some limits and ground rules; or to walk away from a partner that seems unable to treat you with respect, of course.

Dealing with bullies is not easy because they don't think that they are doing wrong, so even if you decide to give them another chance setting some limits, they might not respect your ground rules. Still, your call. You can always walk away at a later point.

Bullying is a stage of abuse, but a bully doesn't necessarily go all the way bad and become an abuser. The difference is the intent:

● While bullies might not care about your feelings, they also don't believe that what they are doing has a detrimental impact. It's the 'c'mon it's not so bad!' belief.

● Abusers know that they are hurting you, which is why they are doing it: They are set to punish you.

I find that when we talk about bullying at school or at work, we miss that bullies will behave this way indiscriminately, in other words, they will be the same for everyone because they don't feel that they are doing something so wrong. This is the point were the school, or the management at work, have the opportunity to stop the environment from becoming a bullying culture: If there is a complaint, something must be done.

That is because a bully will not magically learn that certain behaviours are unacceptable.

If the school gives the child (and parents) a warning of suspension, or the management at work does give the person in question a warning of consequences, the first time, then the bully will have the choice of stopping abusive behaviour, or accepting the consequences.

The problem starts when there are no consequences.

In relationships it works exactly the same way: If you don't tell your partner that he or she is hurting your feelings, you are depriving your better half of the chance of changing attitude towards you. Therefore, you cannot expect them to magically come up with it, which is NOT the same as to say that it is your fault that it is happening.

But always understand that:

It is never your fault what the other person **chooses** to do.

They are free to choose differently.

And that is the beauty of being born in this time and age: People is free to choose.

Still, communication is key in relationships, and let's not forget that bullies don't naturally know when they are doing wrong, therefore first step should be saying 'I don't like that, please don't do it'. At which point you are testing what exactly it is that you are dealing with, bottom line being **it needs to stop because you asked for it**.

If it doesn't… You deserve to be with someone that is able to treat you better than this person.

There is your consequence.

Spotting Abuse

Unlike your average bully that behaves the same way indiscriminately, abusers tend to target particular people and do their best to hurt them in anyway that they can think of, knowing perfectly well what they are doing, and feeling good about themselves doing it.

You can even say that they are almost proud of what they are doing to their victims since they have convinced themselves that it needed to be done because their victims deserve it.

Abusers intend to hurt**.**

And so since they have convinced themselves that you deserved it, they don't have to feel bad for the damage they cause you. They transfer that responsibility to you, for deserving it. At least in their mind.

Abusers are utterly incapable of taking full responsibility for their actions without excuses, scapegoats, or blaming others. They simply cannot comprehend the concept of Accountability. So when you hear them saying, 'You made me do it, this is your fault!', they actually believe it.

And you are not going to be able to talk sense into them, **they do not have the capacity to understand that no one would, nor could, force anyone to abuse them**; you will not convince them of the impossibility of it. That battle is lost. Entering it will only consume you.

But knowing who you can reason with, and who you can't, is only useful if you already know and accepted that things are not how they are supposed to be in the relationship. That means that you have recognised already that unacceptable behaviour is taking place.

As we said before, name calling is one of many things that shouldn't be taking place, as well as mockery of flaws or defects, or continuously provoking arguments against you.

On top of things, abusers are big in manipulation, setting you up to fail, purposely misleading you to trip you over through half truths or blunt lies, … And none of that is acceptable because it is disrespectful, premeditated, and it causes harm, which they are very well aware of. Still, they will feel it is OK to do all of those things to you in order to punish you.

Remember here that, from the abuser's perspective, your role in the relationship is to submit and/or to be punished.

And while we are at it, let me point out that **your partner does not have a birth right to punish you**. That honour stays with the qualified authorities like a judge, or the police, when you commit a crime. Full stop.

So if you are being punished on your relationship, you might want to consider at this point whether you want a relationship based on support (which is what relationships are for), or you want to live with your enemy, knowing that it is NOT supposed to be that way.

What About Support?

In a relationship, as a rule, you are not supposed to work against each other, you are supposed to support each other.

But the funny thing about this is that you cannot support who you cannot respect, which reinforces the importance of respectful behaviour.

Don't be surprised if in a relationship where there is no respect, ideas, plans and suggestions get dismissed immediately. They won't be considered. And that is because without respect for you, nothing that comes from you can be respected either, which means that supporting any of it would be as much as entertaining nonsense; in other words: Inadmissible.

So let me ask you, have you ever felt that whatever you ask, the answer is always no?

That only happens when the person that is constantly denying you will not consider anything coming from you. This person does not want to hear your ideas, does not value your input, and is not in the least interested in what you may have to say. You might as well be talking to a wall.

Let's note that:

Nullifying your input is unacceptable behaviour, and it comes from disrespect for your value in this relationship.

You cannot expect support from someone that thinks so little of your value.

At the same time, you cannot make people value you: They either do or they don't.

What you CAN do is to **understand that you should be valued**, and that it is not your fault if you aren't. It is the other person's choice.

And the bottom line still remains: You cannot change what others choose to do, but you can choose not to accept their failures towards you.

More Unacceptable Traits

Check these out:

● Belittling, or making you feel insignificant.

• Demeaning, or humiliating you.

• Intimidation.

How often do any of those instances happen in your relationship?

The correct answer is: It shouldn't happen.

They are expressions of hatred, and are done with the purpose of submitting the other person, as in forcing them to feel they are less than you.

It is no longer about having a bad day and being irritable with those around us, it is about putting someone down to the point that they loose their will to yours.

For a starter, you should never ever feel intimidated by your partner. Full stop. That should never happen.

Let's have a look at this testimony, for example:

'Years ago I was in the car with my partner at a time. He was driving. There was no visible traffic, and so he thought it would be hilarious to go on to the oncoming traffic lane, just a few yards before a turn.

'I literally stopped breathing. And all that time he was laughing. I thought he had gone mad.

'He did that out of the blue, randomly, while we were just quietly going home one evening.

'We spent the rest of the way arguing, me mostly screaming and him dismissing the gravity of what he had just done. He thought it was a valid excuse that normally at that time he hadn't seen much traffic on that junction.

'Not for one second he considered that he scared me to the bone.'

Now, going back to the title of this chapter: Is This How It's Supposed to Be?

No, normal people don't drive on the oncoming traffic lane EVER because it is dangerous.

The same way that normal people don't wave hammers or knives at their partners, or act in any other way dangerous, threatening or intimidating.

And it doesn't matter that they will try to dismiss the gravity of any of those acts, and try to convince you that you are being silly, or melodramatic. The fact that they will try should put you on your guard that you are not dealing with a normal person.

People capable of dangerous acts like that tend to be pretty good at making you doubt yourself, which is why you need to block their arguments, and think to yourself: If I was scared, it wasn't right.

Because:

If you are scared, it isn't right!

There is no gray area here.

Is This Love or War?

To recap, normal people don't put you down or mock you regularly. Normal people don't hide things from you to trip you over. They don't say things to make you feel worthless. And they don't ever use you as a scapegoat, or blame you for the bad things that happen to them in life.

If this is happening in your relationship, remember that while your partner is making you feel bad with any or many of those tactics, he or she is not investing time in your happiness.

Far from it.

Normal people talk with you about what bothers them, and listen to you when you speak. They might not agree with you, but they won't just antagonise you and quickly make up some sort of excuse to justify themselves and making you the bad guy or causing you to feel stupid.

And when normal people disagree with you, there won't be any consequences.

If you find yourself not speaking up for fear of consequences, something is definitely wrong.

So this is where I ask you to stop, to have a hard look at what is happening in your relationship, and to decide if you are in a partnership, or a war of attire.

In every relationship there must be respect, balance of power, and there must be points of support. If there aren't, you are being worn out in a cold war.

Now please, ask yourself if this is how you want to live, KNOWING that it isn't supposed to be this way.

Because you deserve better.

Chapter 4: What Is A Psychopath?

Psychopaths are people who are unable to bond with others normally and instead prefer to remain detached. They are likely to feel no empathy for whatever reason, though just like the sociopaths, can be very charming with disarming smiles or conversations. Psychopaths easily manipulate their victims because they know how to gain trust as they can be very loyal when there is a reason to be. Since they have sharpened their wits at mimicry, they can mimic varying emotions even though they do not feel them. They appear very normal to unsuspecting victims and are usually very educated with steady jobs. Most psychopaths are so good at mimicry and can have families or even hold steady relationships without those close to them even minutely suspecting them.

Psychopaths plan all details carefully when they intend to commit crime. Unlike the sociopaths, they ensure all their activities are well calculated before being carried out. Since they are meticulous, cool and calm, they leave very little room for suspicion. In most cases, the crimes they commit are thoroughly organized to leave no clues to the authorities to make pursuit. This excellence in execution of crime applies to both violent and non-violent activities.

Causes of Psychopathy

It is believed that psychopathy is the result of nature or genetics. It has a distinct relationship with that part of brain that controls emotions and impulse. This section may be underdeveloped or may have some defects during the fetal stage, at birth or during the very early days of a child after birth.

Of all social disorders, psychopathy is the worst. This is because psychopaths can carefully disassociate themselves from their actions even when they are very grave. A number of serial killers like Ted Bundy and John Wayne Gacy were very unremorseful of their actions. The notable cortical under-arousal, impulsiveness and fearlessness all lead psychopathic individuals to take risks. They are also unable to internalize normal emotions like affection.

How to Identify a Psychopath

Very uncaring- Psychopaths are naturally callous and do not show empathy. They can be described as being very 'cold-hearted'. They also do not care for others' feelings. For normal people, caring for others is driven by emotions that will drive one to fall in love with a member of the opposite sex, or show compassion for relatives, friends and colleagues. This part is largely lacking in the psychopath. Research shows that this is attributed to the brains having weak connections where the brain's emotional systems are found. The disconnections lead to the inability to have deep feelings for close acquaintances.

Can't notice fear- They have been found not to notice fear on others as well. At the same time, they lack the emotion, which leads to disgust in normal people. A sane person will be disgusted when they see gory pictures of mutilated body parts and decide never to get into actions that could lead them to certain activities that cause pain to others. To the psychopath, there is total indifference when shown pictures of mutilated faces or even when exposed to very foul smells.

Shallow Emotions- Psychopaths show no emotions like guilt, shame, embarrassment and fear. When an experiment was carried out to find the different reactions towards fear between normal people and psychopaths, it was discovered that normal people showed some discomfort when anticipating pain. The psychopaths showed none. Instead, they remained totally indifferent when they were mildly shocked using electricity. Further studies showed the brain remained constant during the experiment in the psychos while it changed drastically in normal people who showed signs of nervousness.

Irresponsibility- Psychopaths are very unreliable. They also do not admit to their mistakes and instead choose to blame others. They only ever admit when pushed to a corner in which case, they show no guilt, embarrassment or remorse.

Falsehoods- Even though they easily win people over, psychopaths rarely or never tell the truth. They can be described as very glib in their speeches with superficial charm. They are good at falsehoods, sometimes inflating or distorting speech to suit their egos. A number of them are good at conning others for pleasure or personal gain. One father with a psychopathic girl had this to say; "The girl can say a lie with a very straight face and does not regret her actions thereafter. After obtaining whatever she needs, she seems to be at perfect peace with herself, no remorse or feeling of guilt whatsoever!"

Overconfidence- Psychopaths are more than confident and that explains why they easily win people over. Most of them boast of huge achievements without any qualms.

Narrowed Attention- Psychopaths have a deficiency of response modulation. In normal people, tasks can be altered depending on relevant information that appears when the tasks have began. Since psychopaths lack this ability, they are impulsive and once they begin a task, they do not alter it for any reason. They are able to perform their tasks perfectly because they cannot be distracted like normal people.

Selfishness- They can be said to love a parasitic lifestyle, not caring for others apart from themselves.

Violence- Psychopaths have very little tolerance for frustration. They are irritable and very aggressive, explaining why they fight or assault others.

No Future Plans- They cannot plan for their future and have no realistic future goals. They live for the moment, not caring what tomorrow brings.

Chapter 5: Sociopath Susie

If you think that Ned is the worst colleague that you have, you haven't met his friend yet. Susie is probably one of the people that you would definitely not want to encounter. The problem is that Susie seems to be well-liked by everyone. What is there to hate? She's well-dressed, successful, intelligent, cultured, sophisticated, and seems to treat everyone well.

What most people do not know about Susie is that most of the things that she tells about her life is a lie — and she is not one bit sorry about having to invent the events in her life to make other people love and/or like her. She is also single most of the time — her exes would swear that she gets what she wants and it does not matter what the method is. She does not care about other people. She does not know how to love. However, she knows how to put up a show.

The Problem With Sociopaths

The real trouble with people like Susie is that they probably make it into the top executive positions of most companies. These people are those who are not afraid to undermine their colleagues in order to get into a powerful position, and they are willing to even take credit for the work that they did not do. They are willing to sabotage anybody who gets into their way because they believe that the results always justify the means. If it means being in the top 1% of the world, they are willing to bribe and steal from everyone.

Sociopaths like Susie are much worse than all the Neds that you will meet in this world because they are not only full of themselves; they also make sure that they have the best of everything, and they will not stop until they have created the picture of success that they have in mind. They are very meticulous about details, and they have the ability to create a "society" wherein they are on the top of the food chain.

Could It Get Worse?

Here is a very important thing that you need to keep in mind: Sociopaths are not psychopaths, but it is often said that sociopaths are simply unrefined psychopaths. Psychopaths and sociopaths are often confused to be the same, since both groups lack any sense of moral compass. However, psychopaths are those that you read in the news — irreligious terrorists, serial killers, school shooters are labeled as psychopaths because they transcend their need to exist in a society. When a sociopath makes the decision that he does not need other people to get power or that they can establish their own social order, then it becomes reasonable for them to lead a life of crime.

What You Can Do?

If you have the chance to walk away from people like Susie, now is the time. This person is definitely not worth being a part of your life or trusting with any investment. They are incredibly deceptive and manipulative, and they will stop at nothing until they get what they want.

However, if the situation can't be helped, what you can do is to be extra mindful of everything that a person like Susie does. It also does not help to think that you can change this person — this person is not interested in how you feel or what you think. This person is only interested in power.

It may also help to tell sociopaths that you are not interested in anything that they have to offer, if it means having to deviate from your own values and cause pain to other people. Since power is the only thing that motivates them, it may be helpful to make them aware that they are not getting it from you. When that happens, they will lose interest in you. Without them breathing down your neck, you will be able to get your peace of mind back.

Chapter 6: How To Spot A Psychopath?

There is a tendency to confuse between a sociopath and a psychopath. However, any resemblance is superficial. They are as different as chalk and cheese. They may behave in a similar fashion outwardly but they are different internally. Their mind functions differently. Their brain chemistry is found to be different.

Psychopaths are extremely ruthless. They can kill without showing normal emotions. They are cold blooded murderers. A very high percentage of criminals in prisons are psychopaths. It is therefore essential to spot and avoid psychopaths. Is the person you are dealing with extremely suave and charming?

Smooth talkers are always suspect. Psychopaths can easily hide their true emotions. In fact they don't feel any emotions like normal people. They are extremely charming when they want to. Sometimes, you may even be surprised when these psychopaths are discovered. However, their smile is plastic and artificial which you can spot if you are watchful. Psychopaths will show cheerfulness without displaying other body language associated with a situation. Since they are inherently not capable of emotions, their behavior is artificial and sometimes even out of sync with the situation. Not all smooth talkers are psychopaths and you should look for other indicators before labeling anyone.
Is that person manipulative?

This is one strong indicator of psychopathic behavior. They are highly manipulative and have the guile and cunning to make you act against your wishes. They are persuasive and convincing. They love to climb up the corporate ladder and will use any trick to reach the top. You can spot a psychopath when they use people and dump them as soon as their task is accomplished. Does this person you are with respond to this description? Psychopaths manipulate everyone – subordinates, bosses, partners and even children. Combined with their lack of emotional quotient, their behavior can become sinister. Such people can be spotted by their repetitive actions of using and throwing away their associates and people around them.

Does this person think too much of himself?

Psychopaths think no end of themselves. They are born narcissists. There is a distinction between a narcissist and a psychopath. All psychopaths are narcissists but few narcissists are diagnosed as psychopaths. Since they are narcissists, they will be seen to preen and groom themselves often. They are prone to boasting about their superior abilities which can be a total give away. These psychopaths can be found in corporate board rooms and you are better off avoiding them. Psychopaths strongly believe that they are superior to others and tend to boss over others by boasting about their accomplishments. Sometimes psychopaths are gifted individuals and therefore it may become difficult to categorize them.

Do they accept responsibility?

Psychopaths will never accept committing any mistakes – ever. They will smartly pass on the blame to the situation, circumstances or other individuals. You will never see them showing modesty. They will never share success. Psychopaths want to occupy the stage on their own.

They want to be the top gun. They will shrug off failure giving umpteen excuses. They will trample on the career of others, if they see an escape from it. They will blame the media, talk about with imaginary enemies and distort facts when they face failure. This trait of avoiding responsibly is ingrained in psychopaths. They are adept at playing the blame game. It's better to avoid them when something goes wrong because you may be victimized for no fault of yours.

Do they have childhood issues?

Psychopathic behavior is ingrained. People are born with this disability. It's in their genes. It is generally accepted that their environment has little to do with their malaise. It is therefore natural that you will find psychopaths from all strata of society. A poor child or a rich kid, psychopaths always commit some kind of deviant behavior during childhood. They may have been caught stealing or behaving in ways which may have got them into trouble with the law. If you dig into the past of a psychopath, you will find traces of abnormal behavior in their childhood days.

Do they behave morally?

Since psychopaths have a different brain structure, they don't have the same moral compass as other normal people. They behave morally only to the extent that they can avoid the law. They consciously remain within the confines of social norms and acceptable behavior. They are cold and calculative. They plan their actions well ahead of any event. Sociopaths can be impulsive and can show passion and anger, but a psychopath will never reveal his true emotions – because he does not feel any emotions in the first place.

Do they display guilt?

Psychopaths who have been caught after committing heinous crimes like cold blooded murder have seen to be totally emotionless. They are impassive and detached when discussing their crime. It's as if they never committed a crime. Psychopath may behave normally after killing someone. They are extremely violent in their behavior but don't show any guilt after murdering another person. They just don't have the nerve which is meant for feeling or showing guilt.

Not only in serious crimes, but even in inconsequential matters, a psychopath will keep a calm appearance. This is one characteristic which should raise a red flag from your side.

Do they lie compulsively?

Lies, lies and more lies. Psychopaths revel in telling lies with a straight face. They lie even when there is need to tell a lie. It's a habit with which you can spot a psychopath. Even sociopaths are compulsive liars. Psychopaths are adroit liars and you will have a tough task nailing their lie. They will give excuses and explanations which will be totally convincing to prove that they have not lied. Psychopaths will never accept that they have lied. If you see a person lying continuously and in situations which doesn't warrant a lie, you should conclude that he may be a psychopath or a sociopath.

Chapter 7: Sociopathy

Sociopathy is greatly misunderstood and misused by non-psychologists. Perhaps it is Hollywood providing hundreds of TV shows and movies about individuals with antisocial personality disorders that have greatly confused the situation or simply the beginnings of determining proper terms and definitions? Actually the truth is in the 1930s behaviorists decided a new term was required for antisocial behaviors on the thought that social situations, abuse, and environment played a greater role in violent tendencies. Behaviorists felt a baby when born was a blank slate. It is an argument that improper nurturing and the environment a baby is in can determine if the person will grow up to have violent tendencies as well as suffer from a lack of emotional connection. When the term was created psychologists found that almost every criminal fit the definition of sociopath. Due to the broadness of criteria assigned to sociopaths, an issue with using psychopath and sociopath has come about. The one thing that makes it possible to still use this term is the genetic studies relating to psychopaths.

It is clear that not all criminals who have violent behavior with a lack of empathy and other antisocial behaviors has a lack of MAOA and other genes that are clearly linked with psychopathic tendencies. A person can lack empathy, not socialize, have anger, and impulse control behaviors. Since it is not linked to genetic factors, but it is often linked with a troubling childhood sociopathy applies. Criminals fitting this pattern have been in a very negative household situation. Often physical abuse, childhood trauma, or emotional abuse has occurred.

There is also a difference in behavior with regards to impulsiveness. A sociopath is usually more erratic, while still intelligent. A sociopath also has issues maintaining a job for the long term as well as keeping a normal family life even to those looking from the outside in. Sociopaths tend to be antisocial in groups and with peers that do not share their same thoughts. A person exhibiting these behaviors can find solace in groups of like-minded individuals, even work in a partnership as long as both have antisocial personality traits or something the sociopath wants.

Typically a sociopath is caught due to impulsive actions that are unplanned or not well thought out. They have little regard for consequences or risks which can occur due to their actions, but they are also unable to control their anger or agitation. When the behaviors increase with significant violent outbursts they are likely to be caught.

Is a Psychopath or Sociopath More Dangerous?

With an understanding of psychopath versus sociopath, where one is born and the other has environmental instances that often lead to criminal behavior it begs the question of whether one or the other is more dangerous. Both certainly present risks to the people around them and society as a whole. Both try to live normal lives while hiding or coping with the disorder they have. However, sociopaths have been known to feel guilt. They may have an emotional disorder that sparks antisocial behavior, anger, and violent tendencies, but their brain is not affected by improper growth of the fronto-temporal lobe or specific genetics. A psychopath feels no guilt because they truly feel a detachment of emotion. A psychopath can kill a cat in the name of a science experiment without feeling any empathy, while a sociopath can feel guilt and remorse for killing the animal.

This dissociation a psychopath has makes them extremely dangerous. They can hide among people, acting normal and behaving with charisma and be social. Several of the famous serial killers like Ted Bundy, Jack the Ripper, the Son of Sam, and the Boston Strangler were psychopaths.

It does not mean that all psychopaths or sociopaths will have criminal behaviors or become violent. It is not a necessary criterion for a diagnosis even for antisocial personality disorder as a main diagnosis. Although it is not required it is more often present than not. Through a discussion of clues to antisocial behaviors and assessing the schools of thought regarding diagnosis, you can understand the two disorders.

Chapter 8: How To Deal With A Psychopath

Of course, dealing with a psychopath is not going to be easy – at least, not at the beginning. Did we not see that a psychopath follows no logic when deciding to act? So, obviously, this is not a person you can reason with. In any case, from what we have already seen, a psychopath is a master of manipulation: using lies and pretence to influence the way you behave towards them.

With that said, you can reduce the damage they bring into your life, or even avoid getting enmeshed in their lives in the first place.

Great principles that can help:

Seek Professional Assistance

A psychopath is one guy who can transform you from one confident and flamboyant person to a withdrawn and unhappy person. This emanates from the tendency of the psychopath to drum negatives onto you. To psychopaths, you are the cause of things going wrong in their lives; and sadly, you seem vulnerable enough to believe it. That unwarranted blame then gets to seep into your skin, your heart, your mind and the whole of you, messing with your personality a great deal.

That mess that has occurred in you as a person can only be undone with the help of a professional. Luckily, psychologists have studied the behavior of psychopaths and your situation will not be new to them, however serious you think it is. They will, hence, show you how to reclaim your person, as you have already been molded into someone else without you realizing it.

One thing you should know is that just as great professionals can be psychopaths, so can great professionals and people of means fall prey to psychopaths. In short, you need not fear stigmatization; it is not your fault you are a victim of a psychopath.

Beware: psychopaths try to make you what they want

Psychopaths want you to look up to them as your ultimate solution to problems; like only they can bring happiness into your life. Well... they messed you up in the first place and it would be great if they could restore your being. However, they want you as their victim forever – bidding their every call. So, for all practical purposes, there is nothing more they want but to enslave your mind.

In fact, if you take the example of cult leaders, it is easy to understand the manipulation of the psychopath, and how, as the victim, you end up locking everyone else out of your life; particularly family and friends. See how one Warren Jeffs led a cult that not only practiced polygamy, but also abused underage girls and boys. Gladly, in this case, some bold victims testified down the line and Warren got a jail term in Utah, US in 2007.

So you can see – once you are aware of how psychopaths work, you can see the manipulation for what it is and stand firm; refusing to succumb to their manipulation. If you had a plan to use a certain route, for example, and you refused to get influenced and alter the route, the psychopath realizes how difficult it is going to be to get you trapped. Often, that will be the end of that attempt as the mouth of the psychopath is always watering, longing for easy prey. If you are informed and wise in the ways of the psychopath, the culprit will give up and leave you alone.

Do not be generous with information

Ever heard of the analogy of someone throwing you the rope with which you hang yourself? That is what happens with psychopaths and their pretentious concern for you. They use that feigned concern, sometimes in a dramatic way, to get information out of you. And then it is hallelujah as the psychopath uses the same information to manipulate you.

If, for instance, you volunteer information that you had some misunderstanding with your mum or dad, the psychopath takes that information and paints a picture of parents who loath you. Therefore … Well, therefore, the psychopath will pose as your savior. And down the psychological decline you begin, as you become easily brainwashed to review all your other relationships with a view to ending them. Every bit of information that comes out of your mouth is fodder for the psychopath.

So, if the psychopath is in your life in a way that you cannot ignore chatting with them, keep to facts when chatting, and avoid showing your stand or opinion. This is because it is your stand that psychopaths are out to change to suit them.

Understand the weaknesses and strengths that you have

Why is this important? It is important because the psychopath is already registering your weaknesses so as to capitalize on them. The same psychopath is taking note of your strengths to know the best way to circumvent them when trying to manipulate you.

For instance, right now, you may not need to think long and hard to identify someone who has gone all out to misuse your generosity. Just because you make donations to the less fortunate and you do shopping for your mum is no reason for someone else to manipulate you into buying stuff for them. That is the stuff psychopaths are made of.

Heed your instincts

If your senses tell you something does not feel right about someone, find your way out. If you are still strangers, make haste and purport to have company around or do something just as dramatic; just get out of wherever you are and lose that company.

And in case it is a budding relationship you are having with someone, and your system keeps ticking caution, nip it in the bud before it turns out to be damaging to your person, your life and the people around you.

Drop all contact

If you feel you have been entangled with a psychopath and you want to sever contact, suppress your urge to call even that once in a while to say hello. Do not even send text messages. In case you send those, the psychopath will jump onto that concern you have just shown and use it to resume the journey of manipulation.

One thing you need to know is that psychopaths have nothing of quality going in their lives. In fact, they are idle for most part, and when they are busy, it is in the business of seeking out victims. Of course, to them, anyone who is not their victim is their competitor.

Do not bother trying to change the psychopath

When it comes to psychopaths, the solution is to part ways. Trying to reform them usually worsens the situation. And if you refer them to a specialist, they leave there wiser and more cunning than before. They do not reform; they only get more ammunition for manipulation.

After all, we are talking of people who are full of themselves, selfish and with no conscience. What professional can really help with conscience? That is a really tall order.

Do not carry any guilt

It would be unfair to you to beat yourself up for falling victim to the psychopath. You were busy leading your normal life, and you had many people to interact with in a positive way, when along came the psychopath unleashing all the manipulation. Since you are a normal human being, you hardly realized that this person was not normal but a psychopath and a leech.

Get informed

The more information you get regarding the thinking and behavior of a psychopath, the better for your recuperation process. You will come to terms with the reality that it is not that difficult to fall victim to a psychopath when you have not come across one before. You can easily get apt information from books on psychopathic tendencies; videos; and also movies.

And how will information on psychopathic tendencies help?

You will understand:

What characteristics of yours made you vulnerable at the onset

The whole process and how the charade continued the whole time

The tactics the psychopath used to keep you toeing the line

The reason you fell for those tactics

Once you understand the whole process, you will feel a sense of freedom. And that is the only way you will be able to undo the psychological damage done to you by your experience in the hands of the psychopath.

Set your conscience free

It is easy for you to ask yourself why it is you could not see the manipulative tendencies, and that brings about a great weight that comes from blaming yourself. You need to stop blaming yourself for not seeing through the psychopath's charade because the best way to catch a thief is to send one.

Now that you are not a psychopath, how would anyone have expected you to have identified one on the spot? So the personal blame is not warranted and you need to allow yourself a fresh start.

Chapter 9: Defying And Acting Against Manipulative Interests And Actions

The cycle of manipulation is not easy to get out from. The impacts it exerts on one's life and even health are traumatic. Indeed, the human mind and psyche is a deep mystery that baffles even the most intelligent psychologists of our time. However, this doesn't mean that you and I cannot do anything to fight against it, stand up to start our lives again, and prevent ourselves from becoming victims of this hated scheme, even if we don't have a background in psychology. The tactics presented in this chapter aim to teach the readers of this book on how to resist manipulation and avoid becoming a victim of this pernicious cycle.

1. Ask yourself this, "Are you being manipulated"?

As previously mentioned, all are susceptible to manipulation, although there are some who are more likely to be manipulated, due to a particular set of attributes. More about these traits shall be discussed in this chapter. On the other hand, it is quite difficult for experts, and the victims themselves, to realize that people whose mindset and behaviors are not that easily exposed to and affected by manipulative actions of others, have their strings being pulled incessantly by opportunistic manipulators. It is important that you know, or possibly have a strong inkling, that you are indeed being manipulated.

So what are the signs that you've got yourself caught in a manipulator's web of deceit and mind games? Surely, if this is a serious enough a situation to garner attention from psychological experts, there are tell-tale signs that the worst is actually happening. These are the manipulator's fluctuating personalities, the physical, emotional and psychological impacts of the manipulator's control on your life, and the dynamics of the relationship and environment that you share with the manipulator.

Manipulator's personality

Most manipulators, as already mentioned, are expert chameleons. If there is any constant trait they have, it is their tendency to control, abuse and use people without remorse (intentionally or unintentionally), to get what they want. A manipulator's personality changes with any given situation, if that means that he/she will get closer to his/her goals. Oftentimes, it starts with being charismatic, charming and agreeable. At this stage, the manipulator is trying to establish his/her influence by getting to the good side of his/her target, and gaining that target's trust and confidence. The nearer he/she gets to his/her goal, the less he/she needs his/her target, and the more he/she becomes vicious in attitude. If the target tries to remind the manipulator his/her promises, the manipulator becomes hostile and unreasonable. If you see this trend in a person's personality, and you feel it in your guts that you're being used, then there's a high possibility that you're manipulated.

Manipulation's Impacts on Life

The negative emotions stirred by the knowledge that you have been manipulated are enough to cause you stress and depression. A manipulator is known to use anger, hostility, unreasonable moods, intimidation, and in some cases, blackmail, to cause embarrassment, destabilize focus and calm thinking, and instill fear to his/her targets. Fear of scandalous confrontation, conflict, and unhealthy arguments with the manipulator makes the target in constant worry (especially about when and where the confrontations will happen), resulting to mental and emotional stress. These types of stress manifests as well in the physical body, usually as pain (commonly in the gut), headache, too much or too little appetite, high blood pressure, muscle spasms, fast heartbeat, and even seizures.

Dynamics of Relationship and Environment

The relationship's failure or success is defined by its capability to satisfy or gratify both members of the relationship. However, if a bit of manipulation is added as an ingredient, the symmetry and harmony of the recipe of a good relationship is lost, and what's left is a purely unbalanced taste in the mouth.

Influence and persuasion is common in all relationships. For instance, your partner tells you to try the music or food that he/she likes once in a while, so that you can experience what he/she has experienced. This is just a healthy social influence, because sharing is emphasized and persuasion or influence is being done without interfering with the other person's integrity, rights and freedom to choose. However, if the partner wishes to change the other party without respecting his/her choices, resorting to verbal or physical abuse and emotional blackmail, then this is already manipulation.

Most of the time, even if the partner has a strong gut feeling that nothing's going right in his/her relationship with someone controlling, he/she is hesitant to ask for help or get out completely from the relationship. He/She probably thinks that his/her worries are groundless, that it's all in the mind. This may be true, but then, there's nothing wrong from checking the situation thoroughly again to find out the truth. From Harriet Braiker's own list, provided is a table of questions which are indicative signs of an ongoing manipulation in a relationship. The sum of the rates shall evaluate your relationship as manipulative, slightly manipulative (or leaning to a manipulative relationship) and

non-manipulative.

partner?		
Do you think that no matter how happy you made your partner, the good feelings don't last for too long?		
Do you feel that you're working too hard on this relationship compared to your partner?		

Score Evaluation: 120 – 150 (Manipulative Relationship), 100 – 119 (Developing Signs of Manipulative Relationship), <99 (Non-Manipulative Relationship)

2. Evaluate yourself. "What is your baseline?"

Manipulation is a two (2)-party process. Its effectiveness is largely dependent not only on the manipulator's deceit and control, but also on the manipulated's integral weakness. In a manipulative relationship, it always takes two (2) to tango. According to Braiker, a manipulator assesses the target's goals (the things that you like to accomplish), fears (the things that you don't want to lose) and personalities (traits that make a person vulnerable to manipulation), and designs the strategies to set up a manipulative web trap.

If you're being manipulated, then you're partly at fault. It is effective on you because you have manipulation-susceptible properties. It is highly important that you evaluate your whole self in order to find out those properties. Evaluation is done by identifying your baseline, and assessing the issues or situations you're undergoing and your common responses to them.

Identifying your baseline

Who are you? What are your strengths and weaknesses? What are your personalities? What are your dreams and goals? What are your fears? What makes you work hard? These elements determine your baseline, your normal state, and they tell a lot about how susceptible you are to being manipulated. Listing these down will help you better assess your baseline, see the difference in yourself before and after being manipulated, and design a counter-attack or protective scheme against the manipulator's further influence. A sample is given on the next page.

Note: This is considering that you have been or are being manipulated.

Typical targets

Now that you have been reminded of your normal self with the list that you've done, it's time to spot those things about you that are possibly vulnerable to manipulative tactics of other people. The

89

following are the usual types of people

targeted by manipulators.

	even if they're obtained in illegitimate ways
Frugal people	Easily tempted with bargains that are too good to be true
Masochistic people	Accept the cruelty taken out on them, believing that it is just, and that they deserve it

Manipulation can work its curse anytime in someone's life, but there are instances or situations when it is most likely to occur. These periods usually involve greater emotional and psychological investment, more frequent stress, a grander redefinition of identity, and a larger opportunity to gain or lose something important. Like small animals are always on the lookout for predator attacks, people are highly vulnerable and must be in constant guard during these times. These periods include:

Period of transition and significant change in life, career, family and home, age (adulthood), etc.

Suffering a terrible loss (person, job, property, etc.)

Time when great decisions are to be made

Time of uncertainty or instability

3. Accept who you are.

Being TRUE to yourself means understanding not only your strengths, but your weaknesses and needs as well. Your strengths, fears, weaknesses and ambitions define you as a target of a manipulative people. Knowing and accepting them is key to understanding what makes you vulnerable and how you can strengthen yourself more (develop strengths, improve weakness, eliminate fears), in order to become more resistant to manipulative tactics.

4. Do defense as an act of offense.

Manipulators, especially psychopaths, are smart people. Recent studies even concluded that psychopaths' brains are biologically different compared to normal people, and that they are generally more intelligent than the average. Beating them in their own game is not impossible, but it's difficult, and rather, very dangerous. Choosing to play with them is like asking for more trouble. You must be ready to invest a lot of yourself if you decided to go with this choice.

The safest way to deal with manipulators is by starting the change with yourself. Strengthening your mind and emotions is the best attack against manipulators. Remember that these people are control freaks. Their leverage against you consists of just a few, but specific and effective, weakness or fear. They use this weapon again and again, because you're giving them the results that they expect and desire.

For example, if your manipulative partner threatens to leave you whenever you fight and argue, why not give him/her just that? What would be his/her reaction when you say, "Ok, I've had enough of this, I'm out"? This will definitely surprise, or even threaten, your partner. This is something which he/she didn't expect. If you're lucky, he/she will ask for forgiveness, and both of you can talk it all out. However, if he/she remains unreasonable and just as controlling as before, then it's high time you say goodbye, and get on with your life without that person.

Alan Turing said that violence is good because it gives satisfaction. Remove that and it becomes nothing. Likewise, if you deny the manipulators the response that they're expecting, you'll successfully thwart their plans, and possibly discourage them altogether from continuing to manipulate you.

Chapter 10: The Sociopaths: Main Characteristics And The Way They Operate

Many writers, journalists, and the general public confuse a sociopath with a psychopath. These two anti-social personality disorders are very different. Unlike a psychopath, a sociopath is able to feel some empathy, even love. Sociopaths have the ability to feel shame, while psychopaths do not. They are also not conniving or calculative, which a psychopath is at all times. They lack the self-control of a psychopath as well. What makes them similar is that both are manipulative and can be dangerous.

Before we go any further, it is first necessary to identify if your partner is a sociopath. How can you tell? Sociopathy is one of the most complex psychological disorders, as it is not limited to one single trait, but rather presents itself as a syndrome. Sociopaths have no regard for others' feelings. Though they are antisocial, they must not be immediately thought of as criminals. Not all sociopaths work against social norms. Rather, they are often very prominent figures, who uphold the law in front of others without fail.

The sociopath is a charming, intelligent and very eloquent individual. They are popular amongst friends and colleagues and can monopolize the conversation. They do this with great stories about their lives, or even jokes. They are known to entertain a crowd and leave a good first impression. Most people have a positive opinion of them, unaware of their sociopathic tendencies. Sociopaths use their knowledge and charm to manipulate those around them. They will also lie in a relationship to not lose fights, keep their needs and demands above anyone else's and manipulate others to do their bidding.

Below are the main characteristics that will help you determine whether you are, in fact, dealing with a sociopath.

They are popular individuals.

Sociopaths have a group of close friends, which idolize them. This group of friends trusts them and believes everything they say. These people have been manipulated and to some extent brain-washed. The sociopath uses this group to achieve specific goals or have their needs met. These may include money, home, or a positive reputation. As with all anti-social disorders, sociopaths view people as tools or objects. Each person serves a purpose. They use this popularity as a mask as well. They can hide in this group, and use these people to speak on their behalf when attacked or accused. Their friends fully believe the sociopath, to the point that they would defend them even if the sociopath is clearly at fault.

They are expert story-tellers and habitual liars.

People with this disorder have a need to embellish everything they say. When telling a story, they will lie in such a way that even the most illogical story will seem possible. These lies can be used to manipulate the audience, or simply to exalt the sociopath. When telling these tales, they make sure that no one listening was present at the actual event. This is because while their stories hold some truth, the rest is fabricated. Since no one was there, no one can actually claim that they are lying. If someone does bring evidence to prove otherwise, the sociopath will become aggressive, sometimes to the point of violence.

They are reckless and irresponsible.

While most sociopaths are highly intelligent, they are also irresponsible. This may mean that they cannot keep a steady job, or be financially responsible. They disappoint those around them on a regular basis. Naturally, when confronted they offer excuses and blame, but never remorse. This may also be connected to the fact that they have no concern for the emotions of others. They are also reckless to the point of harming themselves. This is interesting as they view themselves as superior or as more important than others. In a way, they are capable of disappointing themselves as well. This may be due to their inability to plan ahead. At some point, they lose control of their reckless idea because they don't think things through. When problems arise, they have no solution. They often put their family and friends in the middle of these careless ideas. Most cult leaders have been known sociopaths. They would also start with an idea that was not well planned. That would cause the idea to crumble, and the sociopath to lose control. In these cult cases, that would often end with mass suicide.

They don't have a conscience.

They have a lack of understanding between right and wrong. This means that most sociopaths engage in some form of criminal activity. Due to their manipulative skills and eloquence, they often commit fraud. They will also steal but rarely for financial gain. Sociopaths can also be aggressive and violent. They have short tempers and little regard for the consequences. When confronted by their loved ones, or by the law enforcement, they have an explanation for everything. They again either fabricate the truth masterfully or blame others for their crimes. Their inability to learn from their mistakes even when punished makes them repeat offenders.

Sociopaths are often unable of having long-term relationships. They become involved with a partner easily, but they rarely stay in a relationship for long. They can, however, form an attachment to another person, but not in a normal way. They will be kind and empathetic one day, and distant another. Their interest in another person comes and goes on a daily or weekly basis. That being said, they can have committed relationships, even get married and have a family.

The beginnings of a relationship with a sociopath.

Sociopaths are usually introduced to their potential partners through family and friends. This is another way that their popularity works in their favor. Their friends can vouch for them. The sociopath is also very charming and can create an ideal image of themselves. They can read a person's needs and wants so well that they can act them out at will. Their great first impressions grab the interest of the possible partner. The beginning of the relationship is always filled with love and excitement. The sociopath may even feel that way about their partner. The sociopath will be kind, loving and attentive. At this point, they gain the full trust of their partner.

The actual relationship.

Once the relationship is secure, the sociopath suddenly changes. They are no longer devoted, kind and loving towards their partner. They become impatient and bad tempered. As with all anti-social personalities, they begin to abuse and degrade their partners. Although the abuse of a sociopath is usually verbal, it can be physical. While this is happening, the sociopath continues to manipulate their loved one. The sociopath may convince their significant other that they are, in fact, the victim. It is not uncommon for the partners of sociopaths to apologize without cause. They show some form of affection throughout the relationship but on irregular basis. This leaves their partner always wanting more and hoping they will change. The loved ones of a sociopath continue to hope that they will reach the good side of their partner.

The end of a romantic relationship.

A sociopath feels no remorse. They have a grandiose view of themselves and are incapable of realizing their mistakes. When a romantic relationship with a sociopath ends, it always leaves the partner destroyed. This is because whatever the outcome, whoever leaves first, the sociopath has no remorse. They behave as if their loved one never existed. Most people try to get some closure but are instead left with nothing. The sociopath takes no time to grieve over the loss of a relationship. They just move on to the next person. This is particularly complex when children are involved. Usually, the sociopath will leave them behind in the same manner. It is much harder, however, to convince a child that their parent is broken and that they are not to blame. A sociopath always leaves lasting scars on those who loved them.

The sociopath is a reckless and irresponsible individual. They are masters of manipulation with no remorse for the damage they cause. They lie about their lives constantly, and if found out – deny and attack the accuser. There is no way to show the sociopath the negative side of their actions. While they do feel and are capable of some love, they can never love anyone more than themselves. Sociopaths manipulate and con their way through life. More often they are harmful on an emotional level. However, there have been cases where sociopaths posed a danger to the masses. Sociopaths can be well adjusted and successful. However, they can never have a normal relationship with others, romantic or otherwise. If you're involved with a sociopath, they have to be willing to change for the relationship to work.

When You Find Yourself In A Relationship

With A Sociopath

Being in a relationship with a partner who is sociopathic is indeed a very difficult experience. A lot of times people find it hard to trust their partners again after they get hurt. And with sociopaths, you are doomed to get hurt a lot if you let your guard down. But relationships cannot exist with walls. If you have to tiptoe around your sociopathic partner all the time, you will hardly be able to invest in the relationship. Good news is, it is possible to make a relationship with a sociopath last long, as long as you have some strategies to defend yourself.

While it is not easy, being in love with a sociopath can also become satisfying, as long as you manage to find the right balance in your relationship. You will definitely need to remember that your partner is a sociopath, and not doubt yourself. A lot of times people end up believing that their partner might be capable of love and show morally acceptable behavior, but this may never come true. The end result is not so pretty. You must avoid falling into the usual traps and stay vigilant.

Apart from that, there are several strategies that you can use to defend yourself:

Remember that they usually have no conscience.
This is one of the hardest facts to digest in

a romantic relationship with your sociopathic partner. You feel love and affection; you want to connect with your partner. However, sociopaths feel none of those. That can be very heartbreaking. But you need to see this differently. For most of us, love means something different based on what we perceive as standards. Standards set expectations, and if we come up short we feel guilty. For sociopaths, there is no need for any standard except the question "what do I want right now?" Beyond that, they will never questions their motives. They constantly keep changing decisions, as they are carried by their momentary whims. You will have to accept this, and take it in stride. It will definitely be tough, but if you set your expectations according to what your partner is capable of, you will handle it better.
Do not believe in their flatteries. Sociopaths are often interested in dominating over people who are down

and have low confidence. When we feel stressed, we seek compliments – and this is where the sociopath is going to strike. Do not believe in what your partner says. While it is really nice to receive compliments, flattery will often create a sense of disillusionment. Sociopathic partners often offer flatteries to their victims to manipulate them. When you see your partner being extra affectionate or charming, make sure that you pay close attention to what they are trying to do. This way you can avoid traps that have been laid out carefully.
Respect yourself.
In her book "The Sociopath Next Door" Martha Stout, an American psychologist, discusses the reasons why we respect others, especially sociopaths. Should you respect others out of fear? Or should you respect them for knowing what is right from wrong, and because they help others instead of manipulating them? We are often taught to stay respectful and not

confront people because of their actions. However, if someone is trying to hurt you and emotionally abuse you, you must show confidence and stand up for yourself. Should you confront your sociopathic partner? Should you fight back or seek help from your family and friends to keep you grounded? The answer would vary depending on the circumstances. You must respect yourself to know that the way you are being treated is not fair. You must be assertive. This way, your partner will not be able to victimize you. The moment you become the victim is when you lose the power in the relationship. Don't let your emotions fool you. While your sociopathic partner may not feel love the same way you do, how can you stop yourself from being naively in love with him or her? It is quite difficult to be in love with someone and be blindsided by his or her deceits. When in love, our brains release a neurotransmitter called oxytocin. This is nature's way of creating a bond between our offsprings and us. We are chemically affected, and then when we discover we have been lied to, our brains undergo shock. The brain stops responding properly in such a situation, even though we are still in love with our partner. We cannot follow logic, and end up feeling desperate. This gives the sociopathic partner more opportunities to gain control over their lover.

The best strategy here is to try and stay as mentally alert as possible to what is happening. While you may feel love for your partner, you need to keep your brain sharp. Pay attention to your instincts, and expect that there will be a lot of pitfalls that you have to avoid.

Relationships with a sociopath become a hazard to our well being only when we let them become toxic partners who can hurt us the first chance they get. But if we adequately defend ourselves from their tactics to manipulate and control, we can do much better to strike a balance that is necessary to maintain an effective relationship with them.

Chapter 11: Symptoms Of A Psychopath

There are many signs and symptoms that someone could be a psychopath and these are being used to diagnose psychopath as young as 3 years old. It is only by considering each of these different traits that someone can be identified with this condition though not all of them are required in order to form a diagnosis. Psychopaths may exhibit some or all of these traits.

Displays superficial, glib charm – Psychopaths are often capable of appearing charming and sophisticated. They are attractive to most people who meet them because of this charming personality however, upon closer attention, it is often a superficial action and does not actually convey any level of emotion on a personal or individual level. The psychopath will have a very aloof way of seeming charming without actually connecting with the individual.

Has an exaggerated estimation of self-worth – Most psychopaths will believe that they are better and smarter than others. They feel that no one can match them in anything they do and, as a result, they tend to act out in more extreme ways. They may start to do little things that they know they shouldn't believing that no one will ever be smart enough to catch them or that they never have to worry about someone finding out it was them. This often occurs because these individuals believe themselves to be completely above anyone and everyone else and definitely above the law.

Has a need for stimulation – Everyone likes to have a little excitement in their lives once in a while. A psychopath is definitely no different and will continue to explore different activities and try to stimulate their own intense desire for excitement and adventure, even when they can't achieve it. They will continue to try achieving anything and everything that they want. Because they have no fear there is little ability to achieve true excitement and exciting activities will become less so very quickly.

Is a pathological liar – Psychopaths want to manipulate people and this means they will do anything and everything possible to make you do what they want. They want you to feel inferior to them or simply to believe something that isn't true because they know you wouldn't accept the truth. They lie because they know it's going to help them gain or maintain control over you. When their lying is beneficial to them they will continue to do it and they will continue to manipulate you into thinking that they are right or that they're telling the truth.

Is cunning and manipulative – Once again, a psychopath wants to have absolute control and that means they will manipulate you and do whatever necessary to get what they need from you. This could be anything from telling you that you're not attractive and would never find someone else to convincing you to get into his or her car late at night when something in the back of your mind is telling you it's just not a good idea.

Shows no remorse or guilt over anything – No matter what they do a psychopath will not feel guilt or remorse for it. Even when they kill someone they do not feel any type of remorse. They are capable of manipulating you into believing they feel remorse or even faking these types of emotions, but they will not be capable of actually experiencing the emotion and do not actually understand what it is or what it feels like. They can only emulate what they have seen others do.

Displays a superficial response to emotion – When exposed to emotional displays from another person they will often have a very superficial response to this type of feeling. They will attempt to express reasonable responses (if they desire) but these may seem hollow or without any real feeling behind them. This is because someone who is a psychopath has no way of truly experiencing the emotions they want to convey and therefore doesn't understand how to do so.

Is callus and shows no empathy – Empathy is another emotion that a psychopath does not understand. Being as they do not have these types of emotions personally and do not feel any remorse or guilt for their own actions they will often seem callous towards displays of emotion from others.

This is especially true if they commit any type of crime or if they are uninterested in even appearing to care about an event.

Lives a parasitical lifestyle – A psychopath will rely on others for everything they have. They like to sponge off someone else and they have the ability to do so because of their manipulative abilities. Because they can seduce or con others into taking care of them, supporting them and even loving them, they are capable of simply acting as parasites on those who would otherwise be their loved ones, whether a partner or a family member or even someone who believes themselves to be a friend.

Has poor control of behavior – Though they pride themselves on being completely in control and better/stronger/more capable than anyone else they come across, these individuals are actually very much out of control. They tend to snap for no good reason and will often have dramatic outbursts that they are incapable of even controlling. These could be over anything from minor to major and will often seem to come out of nowhere. They may be violent or they may simply be loud or erratic. They can also last for a long time, as the psychopath will continue to react to situations.

Is sexually promiscuous – Because they have no fear and a desire for adventure and excitement, psychopaths will often be sexually promiscuous, acting in ways that are dangerous to their own health or well being. They are often under the assumption that nothing bad will happen to them and that they don't need to be concerned about anything that would affect normal people. This tends to extend to their sex life, which will often be varied however, they are generally incapable of truly relating to someone during sex and the experience is often impersonal for their partner.

Displayed behavioral problems from early in life – Psychopaths tend to have behavioral problems all their lives. Even as small children they will generally have trouble relating to others and will get into trouble more frequently than other children their age. They will often experiment with danger and adventure in completely unsafe ways that other children their age would not and may be violent towards others be they neighborhood kids or their own siblings or family members.

Has no realistic goals for the long-term – Though just about anyone could tell you what type of goals they have for their future or even something they wish for their future, a psychopath has no true goals. They will not look forward for the rest of their life and will generally live solely in the moment. They don't tend to reach towards any goals but they will have expectations of greatness and believe themselves about to receive everything they want in life without ever having to work for it themselves.

Is impulsive – A psychopath will act out in any way they want and at any time they want. They don't pay attention to things like responsibilities or obligations and don't care what other people think of them or their actions. They will generally act however they want and at any time because they want something and believe they can do it at any time. They are impulsive because they have no way of controlling their own mind.

Is irresponsible – Because they are often impulsive a psychopath is not someone that you can depend upon to be there for important (or even minor) life events. They will neglect to show up for events or important life experiences because they are busy with other things or because they are simply not important enough to them. Remember these types of people will care only about themselves and not about other people or things that are important to those other people.

Will not take any responsibility for his or her own actions – Even when caught and faced with the consequences of their actions a psychopath will refuse to take responsibility. They will not take responsibility for anything negative that may have happened to them and will generally act as though these behaviors are the fault of someone else or that someone else caused them to become the way that they are. They consistently blame others for their behavior because it is easier than taking the blame.

Will not settle in a long term marital relationships, may have been married several times – Though they are capable of falling into normal relationships in order to maintain an appearance of normality this is through manipulation and conning, as these individuals are not capable of experiencing true emotions. These relationships will often fail because of the irresponsibility, lack of emotion and lack of true connection between the individuals.

Will have a history of juvenile delinquency – Because they have little self-control and are often impulsive or irresponsible a psychopath will generally get into a lot of trouble even as a child and may have a record of this through the court system. These types of trouble are often varied in nature and maybe severe or minor. Psychopaths as children may be violent towards others or towards animals simply as a means of experimentation with feelings they do not possess.

Conditional release will have been revoked – If they have been arrested previously they will have spent time in jail or prison because any conditional release will be revoked. They will not be able to abide by the rules or restrictions of others because they believe they are above these things. This results in further trouble with the law and will often land a psychopath right back in jail or prison to serve the remainder of their term.

Shows criminal versatility – Psychopaths will show versatility in their crimes because they are constantly testing themselves and the limits. They will constantly act in new ways and try new things because they have an extreme level of confidence in themselves and will continue to push the limits of what can or should be done. This includes a variety of criminal enterprises from robbery and car theft to murder.

Extreme egotism – A psychopath thinks of themselves first and everyone else second (if at all). They will show extreme egotism, believing themselves to be the most important people in any situation and therefore the only ones that matter. As a result, they will often offend others with their outbursts or with their actions because they have little regard for anything that does not benefit them personally.

Poor judgment and ability to learn from past mistakes – Unlike other people who will fail at something and realize they need to do it differently, a psychopath will act out and continue to do so in the same manner. This will continue even if the activity fails or if they are caught. They do not have the ability to change their ways of doing things to avoid being caught or getting into trouble and will not be capable of learning and advancing through past mistakes.

Ingratitude and inability to be grateful –
These individuals do not feel grateful for
anything that is done for them, as they
believe that they are entitled to these
things. Instead, they tend to act with a
sense of expectation over these positive
things that come their way.

No history of suicide attempts – A
psychopath thinks entirely too highly of
themselves to ever actually attempt
suicide. They do not want to die because
they believe they have too much left to do
and that they can continue to accomplish
even more throughout their lives. Though
they may act in some ways that seem to
say they want to commit suicide, this is
never actually the intent and the individual
will not have any genuine wish to end
their life.

Chapter 12: The World Is Changing, And So Are The Solutions For Passive Aggression

Out in the research and psychology world, there are little to no resources that offer help men heal their own passive aggression. There are almost no blogs or websites that address the passive aggressive person directly, sitting him down and giving it to him straight. Unhappy wives have taken up this task, only to find themselves embroiled in a secondary battle for who is right.... and losing their own time and efforts against his defenses. Often, these wives just dig themselves into deeper trouble, feeling that they are doing the only thing they can.

For wives in this situation, it is important that they know that this is not the only option they have. Up until now, the husband hasn't realized that there is a problem with his behavior. Even when something bad happens and he instinctively knows he was responsible, he holds on to the idea that he is innocent because he doesn't want people to think of him as doing bad things on purpose or being a "bad person." If he could find out on his own that it's time admit to being passive aggressive, and time to find a strong and immediate solution, wives could find themselves in a much happier situation, emotionally. This is definitely a possible idea, if these wives and husbands know where to look for resources HE can use.

A passive aggressive husband who is not helping himself to heal is only promoting more bad situations by avoiding looking at problems directly. His relationships end up sabotaged by his own brain and learned reactions, and in defense mode, he can't admit that there's a problem and work to heal it. So, things just get worse and worse for him - his wife is more threatening and confrontational, he's more defensive, which makes his wife even more confrontational! It's an endless cycle of escalating vicious situations.

The reason why the wife trying to change him isn't working is because most of the time, what everyone calls his "passive aggression" is behavior done by his unconscious brain, reactively. He may not know what he's doing when he does it. That's why it's important for him to stop now and see that he IS doing something with a negative impact. The next step shouldn't be denial but a question to himself: "HOW DO I STOP?" It's also important that he realizes this toxic behavior and its impact on his own (e.g., you can only change yourself, not others) instead of the wife telling him "This is what's going on."

His actions become unconscious because they are learned early on in life. By not trying to identify these behaviors and heal them, he's ignoring his own childhood priming and the HUGE impact of this model of connection on his life even now. The consequences? A constant fear of connecting with his loved ones and bleak, utter loneliness. Not the mention, the sense that something is wrong and threatening, that he should protect himself from it, but never knowing exactly why or what from is always with him. He (and his wife!) can never be happy in that mode!

So where should unhappy wives go from here? There are many resources that a passive aggressive husband can use to identify his childhood lessons and thus own his own passive aggressive behavior.

Remember: whether or not the WIFE knows he's PA, HE also has to come to that realization.

Neil Warner is the main "relationship guru," in his blog where the main focus is to increase the quality of love-based relationship experiences, focusing now on healing passive aggressive behaviors.

In a new, ground-breaking Six-Step System Neil offers a complete program to identify and change this impact of passive aggression in marriages with love and compassion. When there is emotional abuse, or anger issues or marriage conflict, Neil can provide good support and tools to change behaviors, so anybody can overcome childhood patterns that generate unhealthy relationships and be happier.

WHAT CAUSES IT?

No matter what gender someone is or where they have come from, there is likely to be moments where they feel angry. This is part of the human experience and it plays a valuable role in our survival as individuals and as a species.

In most cases, anger is nothing more than feedback and is informing someone that they are being compromised. Their boundaries are being crossed and that some kind of action needs to be taken.

However, this natural and healthy process can end up becoming dysfunctional. And like so many other human aspects; if it is not expressed in a healthy and functional manner.

Anger

And while anger is a word and an experience that most people can relate to, there are many other ways that anger can be experienced that are often not as familiar. These are: resentment, irritation, aggression, rage, depression and hate.

At first it will be anger that is experienced, but over time this can turn into these other experiences. This can be due to a numbers of reasons and one of these reasons is repression.

Here, anger can be covered up for what could be a few days, to a number of years. And instead of it being a momentary experience, it then becomes a state of being.

The Cover Up

This may be something that one engages in all of the time or only ignores their anger during certain times and around specific people. But one thing is clear, and that is although one may do all they can to cover up how they actually feel, it will be observable in some way.

There can be many reasons why someone can feel compromised and therefore angry. Some of these can be the result of feeling: abused, ignored, violated and taken advantage of.

Passive Aggressive

If one doesn't acknowledge how they truly feel and the experience that they are having, it is going to appear in a way that may be dysfunctional and disempowering. And one of the most common ways that this come be known is through passive aggressive behaviour. It could be described as revenge that has been delayed.

This behaviour can be extremely subtle and hard to spot at first. And this has the potential to create frustration and anger in the person who is observing the behaviour.

One Consequence

In some cases, this can lead to one taking on board the anger and frustration that the passive aggressive is not willing to face themselves. Here, one can start to feel angry for no apparent reason when they are around the person. At a conscious level one can be oblivious to this fact, but at an unconscious level, it is being picked up. And confusion then occurs at a conscious level.

But while the observer of this behaviour can feel angry or frustrated, if they were to question the person who is passive aggressive about the role they are playing, they may even dismiss and deny what is taking place. Claiming not to be angry in any way and that the person who is observing this behaviour actually has anger problems.

It could be that they have no awareness of their passive aggressive behaviour. And if one has a pattern of attracting people who are passive aggressive, then they may have some work to do around anger.

Examples

Passive aggressive behaviour can appear in many different forms and guises. And some of these are:

When someone turns up late

When someone forgets to do something

When someone becomes cold or distant

When someone becomes silent

When someone behaves in the ways that have been described above, it doesn't necessarily mean that they are being passive aggressive. These have to be taken in context and weighted up with other sources of information.

Reasons

To be passive aggressive is not a functional way of behaving or a sign of maturity. However, it is there for a reason and the primary reason is that it is what feels safe. We all have an ego mind and what is familiar is what is classed as safe. And to be passive aggressive will be what feels safe or comfortable.

If this person was to act another way, there would be the potential for fear to arise. As to the ego mind, if something is unfamiliar it will be interpreted as the equivalent of death

So if this person was to express their anger in a functional and healthy way, it wouldn't feel comfortable and may even feel dangerous.

The Relationship

For one to express their anger in a healthy and functional way, it will be imperative that they have a healthy relationship with anger. And as anger is often labelled as negative and destructive in today's world, it is common for people to believe that anger is a bad thing.

Childhood Development

One of the biggest influences in the kind of relationship that one has with anger will be their childhood years. If their caregivers dealt with their anger in ways that were generally healthy, it would have been likely that they passed this ability on. And one therefore had healthy models to mirror and internalise.

However, if their caregivers repressed or denied their anger or expressed it but discouraged it in others, then this would have been modelled and internalised. And as a child, ones ego mind would have formed associations around this behaviour being what is familiar and therefore safe. So to behave in another way could cause one to feel: rejected, vulnerable or abandoned for example.

Awareness

Just because something happened many years ago and the mind has forgotten about it, it doesn't mean that it is no longer having an effect. And passive aggressive behaviour is just one example of this.

One may need to seek the assistance of a therapist or healer to release the anger that may have built up over the years. Or to have the help of a coach or a trusted friend in order to express anger in a way that is functional and empowering.

My name is Oliver J R Cooper and I have been on a journey of self awareness for over nine years and for many years prior to that I had a natural curiosity.

For over two years, I have been writing articles. These cover psychology and communication. This has also lead to poetry.

DON'T LET YOUR FEELINGS BUILD UP

In one of the previous chapters, we discussed how to recognize passive aggression, and how the passive aggressive person communicates his or her emotions. Passive aggressive behavior takes many forms but can generally be described as a non-verbal aggression that manifests in negative behavior.

Instead of communicating honestly when they feel upset, annoyed, irritated or disappointed, a passive aggressive person will bottle the feelings up, shut off verbally, give angry looks, make obvious changes in behavior, be obstructive, sulky or put up a stone wall. It may also involve indirectly resisting requests from others by evading or creating confusion around the issue. It can either be covert (concealed and hidden) or overt (blatant and obvious).

A passive aggressive person is keen to avoid show how much is angry or resentful. They will cover up their anger with an appearance of agreement and friendliness by using kind words.

We all shut off sometimes, and keep our feelings bottled up. However, letting that become a normal way of interacting with people (because you've been hurt and can't trust others, or because it's just "easier") can lead you down a dangerous road to passive aggression. Once you make passive aggression, your pattern of interacting with others, it's very hard to keep friends and loved ones close, and you'll find it hard to keep personal connections alive.

Perhaps you think that there is nothing wrong with not showing anger - that it is "zen," "manly," or "stoic." There is nothing wrong, of course, with being in control of your emotions.

There is something wrong, though, with pretending that those emotions don't exist. This passive aggressive behavior, done consistently, destroys trust between friends and significant others.

Ask yourself, what is the purpose of an intimate relationship if you can't show your feelings? Sex? Financial support? Why not just get a hooker or a good job then? Even if you don't want to admit it, emotional connection and support is probably important to you (it's sort of an instinctive need in us humans, actually). You won't be able to get it when you're shutting yourself off passive aggressively, which means hiding your pain (anger, sadness, disappointment) will only actually cause more pain.

It creates negative energy in your partner, who feels that you don't trust them. They get angry at you, and then you get angry at them for being angry, and then you don't express it and withdraw more.... and round and round it goes.

Ask yourself - are you doing anybody favors by pushing your emotions deep down inside?

Aren't you hurting anybody, including yourself?

You may feel that if you express your real emotions you won't be accepted. In this case, you may be in danger of hurting people through passive aggression because you feel that they can't (or won't) love the real you.

This is your low self-esteem talking, and it's time you started talking back.

Next time you're feeling something strong and are going to (once again) pretend everything is okay, kindly open a door in your mind and kick that self-hating voice out onto the street.

Repeat this: "I am a person worthy of love, and I will show it by expressing my emotions in a grown-up and respectful way."

ENDURING THE PASSIVE AGGRESSIVE

Some people cannot help being passive aggressive when life turns a way they don't like which is characteristically most of the time. Actually, we are all tempted to behave in passive aggressive ways. Most of us have engaged in it.

So what is it: passive aggressiveness?

It is covert anger. When someone can't get their own way they resort to resistance even when it appears they are cooperating. They have no intention of cooperating. They have every intention of creating mayhem under a guise. Their smile is really a sneer. Their "Fine, love to help" is really a "Fine! We'll see, buddy." They think pathologically; and negative agenda's continually the pattern.

Many of us have someone in our family or within our workplaces that exhibits this sort of problematic behaviour. No matter what we try they may insist on doing everything they can to bring off the win. Everything is a competition and selfishness is the drive. But they seek the win in ways to not cause enough ripples that we'll attack them back. It's about the scheming undertone of their demeanour.

What can we do to endure them?

ONE IDEA: LOSE WITH GRACE

Yes, lose! Keep reading. When winning is no longer the key to our agenda, and our agenda swings to favour them, we win when they win. But this is not submission. This is actually choosing to take the upper hand; to give them what they want; to rise above the pettiness; to make a heavenly statement of tack by dying to self.

Losing with grace will not be a popular choice of tactic. Many will think we are a pushover, and that's exactly what it looks like. But who has control? Who has made the choice as to how each situation will play out? Who will never become discouraged? Who is to remain cheerful, despite their reaction? Who truly has the power?

Only the mature person can die to self so consistently as to rise above the passive aggressive person and win while the passive aggressive thinks they are winning. So long as winning is not the point to us, and serving the passive aggressive is the point - and better with the purest of hearts to that end - we rise above all our frustration, and we divert our emotional energy into a spiritual exercise of giving all the glory to God.

The sense for victory that we gain in losing at one level but winning on another is a heavenly prospect. Nothing can come close to the blessings of God encapsulated in knowing there is nothing any human being can do to upset us. That is our vision.

HOW TO DEAL WITH PASSIVE AGGRESSIVE PEOPLE WITHOUT AN ACTUAL CONFRONTATION

How to deal with passive aggressive people? Simply, turn your back and walk away. These types of people are just simply looking for a fight and you can be the bigger person and walk away. It may seem difficult to do but once you understand what goes on in the minds of these insecure folks, then it just all makes sense to walk away.

Passive aggressive behavior is often shown when the person is unable to directly attack the cause of their frustration. It may be because the object of his anger is somebody of a higher rank like a teacher or senior officer in the company where they work in and they need an outlet. They will often vent out their anger to the first person they meet or who seems weak in their eyes. Unfortunately, this could be you.

Do not be a victim and learn how to deal with passive aggressive people. The best way to fight back would be to ignore them completely. However, this could enrage them even more and their attacks could turn vicious at any moment. Be calm whenever their hurl their bitterness towards you, remember that their main goal is to make you as pissed off as they are.

People that display passive aggressive behavior often disguise their insecurities in the form of taunts, teases and even back biting. Do not be surprised when they give a cynical or sarcastic remark when everyone else is congratulating you. They are just frustrated with your accomplishment and resort to name calling or teasing.

Many do not know how to deal with passive aggressive people because they simply accept the bullying and fight back with the same tenacity. This will lead into a confrontation and you, the victim, will become just as bitter as the person with the passive aggressive behavior.

Steer clear of them when possible. If you see them charging down the hallway after being summoned in the boss' office, then by all means avoid them. It is likely that they will be looking for somebody to exact their vengeance on and you would not want that person to be you.

One of the more drastic means on how to deal with passive aggressive people is by standing up against them. Making them see you as their equal will make them think twice about going at you again in the future. They will start to show you respect and be friendlier. The down side to this is they might find another person to bully, but hey, at least you are saved.

As we live our lives, we cannot help but bump into sorts of colorful individuals. Now, some of these folks are okay and cool while some could have their unique set of eccentricities. We can welcome those we like into our small group of friends and those we do not get along with into the acquaintances category, whichever you choose.

The trick is knowing how to deal with passive aggressive people to avoid a violent confrontation.

Chapter 13: Coping With Passive Aggressiveness

"Do not answer fools according to their folly,

or you will be a fool yourself.

Answer fools according to their folly,

or they will be wise in their own eyes."

~Proverbs 26:4-5 (NRSV)

Where do we start with passive aggressiveness? It is all around us - in our homes, our workplaces, our shopping centres, and, intermingled with overt aggressiveness, on the roads, too.

Whenever someone is nice to our face yet we know their real intent is to backdoor or confound us, we know passive

151

aggressiveness. And of the more overt forms, this resistance becomes noticeable, especially in the case of certain types of bullying. Although passive aggressive behaviour is sometimes difficult to pinpoint, it can be almost impossible to combat.

Now, we can be sure that passive aggressive behaviour is the behaviour of the proverbial fool-abovementioned. This person has no real interest in love or the common good.

This gives us both important insight and a warning.

EMPLOYING THE INSIGHT OF THE SAGE

Because God's power is for those who work for good - who go into the threshold of love, despite aggressiveness - there is a way of dealing with the confounding behaviour of those that are skilled in passive aggressive responses in life.

But we can only tap into God's power when we are appropriately wily, like a sage.

Only the wise - those employing well considered thought - can deal with the fool. Only the wise can remain calm enough, overall, in the presentation of folly. Maybe it's only the wise that can work with that folly. And wisdom is the much needed response, because passive aggressiveness is everywhere in this life.

This initiates us to the warning, stated straight in *Proverbs 26:4-5*.

ENTERING A WORLD WHERE NO ONE WINS

The fool has it in their heart that if they cannot win, nobody will win.

Everything, for them, appears as a competition. The person who chooses passive aggressive responses in life sees life competitively or it least selfishly and not as a journey for safety and mutual enjoyment.

This is where we are warned. We cannot change them. We are better off to accept what we cannot change. We may bring them gently to account where we are able to, but it would be foolishness to lose excessive energy focusing on that which we cannot change or control.

With people who are passive aggressive we cannot play their game, yet we only get on by playing their game. It appears as an infuriating trap. But there is a way when we take each situation on its merits.

Sometimes we employ a gentle truth to bring reason to the situation, but most of the time we need to be prepared to accept the presence of many lies, and, importantly, not get frustrated or too overwhelmed. God will reward our patience with wisdom, for we are showing wisdom by not falling into a trap. And when we do fall into the trap, we learn, and by doing so we grow in wisdom.

WHY DOES PASSIVE AGGRESSIVE JUST FEEL LIKE AGGRESSIVE?

If we are all striving for balance in our lives, sitting at opposite ends of the spectrum are very different kinds of social personalities. At one end you have the aggressors, who have no filter or any qualms of hurting other people while demanding they be heard. On the opposite end of this gauge you find the quiet, seemingly compliant personality, who appears content to live without emotional outbursts or needs. Nothing is further from the truth and both personalities are coming from a deep place of fear.

The silent person is passive aggressive and although they will not say much, their silence speaks volumes to those who share

155

their world. Somewhere in their past they learned their voice had no merit, thoughts and feelings did not measure up and they came to a place of doubting every feeling and thought they had. Insecurity and fear drives them deep into an internal box, where they slam the lid down tight. In that moment they create what feels like a safe haven, protecting their fragile ego and wounded heart. The cost of maintaining this protection is very dear as they are wary of everything they do, say or put out into the world. Thus, they live in a world where they must live all conversations in their minds over and over, constantly evaluating answers, playing out scenarios, conversations and responses to everything before them. They doubt themselves constantly, affirming all the old messages of having no value. Life becomes a silent, yet scary contemplation while living in a very lonely box, every potential contact or conversation stressful and filled with panic.

Passive aggressive people will partner up with aggressive personalities, in their primal desire to create balance, to have a voice through another, who will makes decisions and emote emotions that they cannot. In order to find the control and stability that all insecure people need, the passive aggressive realizes that by withholding emotional support and connection, they will spark a constant stream of attention, which comforts them, allows them to feel loved and wanted, momentarily.

The aggressive partner will comply but, unfortunately, this union is a recipe for disaster as the aggressor needs validation they will not get and the passive aggressive will be constantly reminded of their inadequacies. Meltdowns and explosions by the aggressive partner will send the determined passive aggressive person deeper into their box, ensuring no one can get in but needing attention, will

157

seek it in the only way they know, as ferociously as the aggressive partner. The worst thing you can do to a passive aggressive personality is to ignore them, which seems contrary but is the truth as it validates their greatest fears, that they are not worthy of acknowledgement.

The journey to finding balance in our lives, must always come from an act of courage. The passive aggressive person must walk the same path as the aggressive, which is facing their deepest fears, acknowledging the old tape with misguided messages and then taking steps to shed this belief.

If you want to help the passive aggressive person in your life, have patience and be supportive but do not fill the void with the words or decisions that must come from the person in the box. Love unconditionally and allow this person to find their truth, find their words because "not making a decision, is making a decision" and until they change their minds you will have to accept them exactly the way they are. The only person you can really change in the relationship is yourself and when you move to the middle of that gauge, you leave room for the passive aggressive personality to lift the lid of that box, peek out and feel safety in the space between you and them. Space to bring their thoughts and words to the table when they are ready to place their vulnerability before you and the world.

WHICH IS HEALTHIER?

There it is happening again... something has set you off. But, should you hold it in, and risk becoming a negative person, as is the case with passive aggressive behavior, or should you let it out. This is a scenario most people encounter on a frequent basis, some handle it better than others. But, the question still remains... are you better off suppressing your anger, or is being aggressive the way to go?

Aggressive people tend to be more open, so to speak, with their feelings. They do not hold their feelings back at all. At times they may even come across as too aggressive and intimidate anyone around them. Some form of anger management would not be a bad idea in this situation.

What anger management does is help you to recognize when you are angry, first and foremost. Once you are aware of being upset, the hard part is choosing what to do next... and it is a choice. Should you suppress, express, or control yourself?

Unfortunately most people who have issues with anger, completely bypass that step and react abusively. Anger management allows you to realize that expressing your emotions by talking it out, and suppressing violent feelings is more beneficial. This can be a deep process, but once you have mastered control over your emotions, you will find it easier to keep from throwing something or punching someone in the mouth no matter how tempting it may be.

Those who are aggressive wear their emotions on their sleeve and are always on the defensive...this is why many come across as hot heads, and anything sets them off. For this reason, aggressive people also have a higher success of controlling their anger when compared to someone who is passive aggressive.

Why?

Well, simply because aggressive people tend to be more predictable, which helps them to recognize what pushes them over the edge. In contrast, passive aggressive people seemingly hold things in, and in turn may become resentful. Once feelings are held in for too long, they either get buried or are expressed in ugly ways which makes it more difficult to figure out the initial cause.

By knowing what triggers any feelings of anger in the first place, a passive aggressive or aggressive person is more equipped to make better decisions in finding a middle ground between being assertive and aggressive.

It is important to point out, that being aggressive should not be confused with being assertive. Aggressive people are more forceful or demanding. Assertive people take control, while being respectful of others. Respect, is the defining term here.

HOW TO HANDLE A PASSIVE AGGRESSIVE PARTNER

Passive-aggressive people act passive, but express aggression covertly. They're basically obstructionist, and try to block whatever it is you want. Their unconscious anger gets transferred onto you, and you become frustrated and furious. Your fury is theirs, while they may calmly ask, "Why are you getting so angry?" and blame you for the anger they're provoking.

Passive-aggressive partners are generally codependent, and like codependents, suffer from shame and low self-esteem. Their behavior is designed to please to appease and counter to control. You may be experiencing abuse, but not realize it, because their strategy of expressing hostility is covert and manipulative, leading to conflict and intimacy problems.

Personality Disorder

According to the American Psychological Association passive-aggression was considered a personality disorder in the DSM-IV:

This behavior commonly reflects hostility which the individual feels he dare not express openly. Often the behavior is one expression of the patient's resentment at failing to find gratification in a relationship with an individual or institution upon which he is over-dependent. (APA, 1968, p. 44, code 301.81)

After nearly 40 years it was dropped in 1994. There's renewed interest in studying passive-aggression. Passive-aggression was found to be related to borderline and narcissistic personality disorders, negative childhood experiences, and substance abuse.

Characteristics of Passive-Aggression

Because you can't have an honest, direct conversation with a passive-aggressive partner, nothing ever gets resolved. They say yes, and then their behavior screams NO. They try to sabotage your wants, needs, and plans using a variety of tactics.

We all engage in some of these behaviors some of the time, but when there's a pervasive pattern of multiple symptoms, it's likely that you're dealing with passive-aggression.

Denial: Like all codependents, they're in denial of the impact of their behavior. This is why they blame others, unaware of the problems they're causing. They refuse to take responsibility for anything, and distort reality, rationalize, blame, make excuses, minimize, deny, or flat out lie about their behavior or the promises or agreements they've made.

Forgetting: Rather than say no or address their anger, they forget your birthday or the plans you've discussed, or forget to put gas in the car, pickup your prescription, or fix the leaky toilet. You end up feeling hurt and angry.

Procrastinating: They're avoidant and don't like schedules or deadlines. It's another form of rebellion, so they delay and delay with endless excuses. They don't follow through on responsibilities, promises, or agreements. If they're unemployed, they drag their feet looking for work. You may do more job-searching on their behalf than they do.

Obstructing: This is another nonverbal form of saying NO. When you try to decide on where or when to go on vacation, pick out an apartment, or make plans, they find fault with each suggestion and won't offer any of their own.

Ambiguity: They hate to take a stand. They don't say what they want or mean. However, their behavior tells the truth, which is usually NO. This way they retain control and blame you for being controlling. As you might expect, negotiating agreements, such as in a divorce or child visitation plan, is exasperating. In addition to procrastinating, they avoid being pinned down. They may insist on "reasonable visitation," and label your attempts to specify a predictable plan as controlling. Don't be fooled. This only postpones negotiation when repetitive arguments can occur over every exchange of the children. Alternatively, they might agree to terms, but not abide by them. You can expect to be back in court.

Never angry: They don't express their anger openly. In childhood, they may have been punished or scolded for showing anger, or were never permitted to object. Their only outlet is passive-aggressive, oppositional behavior.

Incompetency: When they finally do what you ask, you likely have to redo it. If they make a repair, it might not last or you'll have to clean the mess they made. If they're helping with house cleaning, their inefficiency may drive you to do it

167

yourself. At work, they make careless errors.

Lateness: Chronic lateness is a half-hearted way of saying NO. They agree to a time, but show up late. You're dressed-up, waiting to go out, and they're "stuck at the office," on the Internet, or watching the game and not ready. Lateness at work or delivering assignments is a self-sabotaging form of rebellion that can get them dismissed.

Negativity: Their personality may include pouting or acting sullen, stubborn, or argumentative. They feel misunderstood and unappreciated and scorn and criticize authority. They frequently complain and envy and resent those more fortunate.

Playing the Victim: The problem is always someone else's fault. Their denial, shame, and lack of responsibility cause them to play the victim and blame others. You or their boss become the controlling, demanding one. They always have an excuse, but it's their own self-destructive behaviors that cause them problems.

Dependency: While fearing domination, they're dependent, nonassertive, indecisive, and unsure of themselves. They're unaware of their dependency and fight it whenever they can. Their obstructionism is a pseudo attempt at independence. They don't leave, but withdraw or withhold intimacy instead. An autonomous person has healthy self-esteem, is assertive, and can take a stand and keep commitments. Not so for someone passive-aggressive. Their behavior is designed to avoid responsibility for themselves and family, and sometimes they depend unfairly on their partner for support.

Withholding: Withholding communication is another form of expressing anger and asserting power passively. They may walk

169

away, refusing to talk things over, or play the victim and say, "You're always right," shutting down the discussion. They're unable to articulate what they want, feel, or need. Instead, they retain their power using the silent treatment or withholding material/financial support, affection, or sex. This undermines intimacy as a way to fight against their dependency.

There are a myriad of other things they might do, like slamming doors, giving away something of yours, or offering you dessert that you're allergic to or when you're dieting.

What You Can Do

Because a passive-aggressive person is indirect, it may be hard to recognize what's going on, but it's essential that you recognize whom you're dealing with. Look for a pervasive pattern of several of the above symptom, and monitor your feelings. You may feel angry, confused, or powerless when trying to get cooperation. If this is a common pattern, you're likely dealing with passive-aggression.

It's important not to react. When you nag, scold, or get angry, you escalate conflict and give your partner more excuses and ammunition to deny responsibility. Not only that, you step into the role of parent - the very one your partner is rebelling against. Don't be vague, drop hints, blame, or allow yourself to pay-back in kind.

Neither be passive, nor aggressive. Instead, be assertive. It's far better to address noncompliance and problems in the relationship directly. Frame it in terms of "We have a problem," not "You are the problem," which is shaming. Don't blame or judge your partner, but describe the behavior you don't like, how it affects you and the relationship, and what you want. If you let your partner come up with a

171

solution to a problem, there's a better chance of resolution.

When you go along with your partner's tactics or take on his or her responsibilities, you enable and encourage more passive-aggressive behavior. It would be similar to nagging your child, but allowing the youngster not to do his or her chores. This takes practice and requires being assertive. Be prepared to set boundaries with consequences. See my blog,"10 Reasons Why Boundaries Don't Work" For suggestions on dealing with passive-aggression, write me for "12 Strategies for Handling Manipulators."

HOW TO DEAL WITH SOMEONE WHO IS PASSIVE AGGRESSIVE

I spent over 20 years dealing with different personalities in the working environment, at home, at school, and in other social settings. I was a teacher, student, co-worker, subordinate, manager, family member. Every person I met was different and even though sometimes I felt like I went through the worse already, the next and the next personality knocked on my "life challenges" door. Of all the behaviors I learned, I found the passive-aggressive character trait to be most difficult, delicate and requiring a high level of negotiation and assertiveness skills. I did not know from day one how to deal with it, I actually reacted the same way as the other person, by being passive-aggressive myself. It did not serve me well, so now, years into personal development, training and practice, I wish to share some thoughts on this matter with you.

Whenever you suspect such a behavior, I recommend looking at yourself and most of all, how you communicate. The purpose of this exercise is not to validate of excuse the passive-aggressive under any circumstances. We know that their behavior is definitely unhealthy, non-productive and sometimes even spiteful.

It is a known fact that we are a fundamental part of the way other people perceive and treat us. But, we can't change others and their ways, we can only change ourselves. And that is the starting point, to see if our style and/or our behavior are in any way contributing to an environment complementary to the existence and further development of the condition.

For someone to be encouraged to pursue revenge, they must recognize something wrong done to them-no matter real or not. It is not about us doing or not doing them any wrong. It is about their feelings and considering our behavior to be unsuitable, improper, discriminating or undeserved towards them. Well, occasionally they are accurate.

Although there are subtly covering up their response, it is still not an excused behavior, but now we have gained an opening for when we try to diffuse the passive-aggressive.

Passive-aggressive are often people who are certain that their lives are controlled by others; unfortunately they are likely to lack the ability, understanding, desire and/or self-confidence essential to be assertive. They do attack, so to diminish the strength of their attacks, one must be as assertive as possible. Most of people with such condition lose their desire to fight when faced with someone who is not going in circles and willingly and honestly comments on their behavior. The reason I am pointing this aspect out is that in most cases, passive-aggressive behavior produces a passive-aggressive reply. We all are responsible for our actions and reactions. We must make a conscious decision to not just react or behave in some fashion because it feels good at a given moment. Life is an array of moments and moments have consequences. By making the right choices, our consistent behavior will serve to build up relationships rather than to destroy them.

Passive-aggressive individuals are unfamiliar with being held responsible for their conduct. Be positive as you exercise your counseling, but be ready for an offense at any time.

For example, the best assertive response to a passive-aggressive person who openly disagrees with you in public would be, "Thank you. I appreciate your willingness to tell me how you feel face-to-face."

Never doubt that passive-aggressive individual is at war with you. In order to improve the relationship with them, we must learn to know how they feel. Unless we know how they feel, we will never be able to plan a successful approach to improve the relationship.

As the person recognizes more of what is expected of them and understands why those expectations are relevant to their future good, the less likely they are to employ in passive-aggressive conduct.As in all situations, not only do they need to understand the expectations but the consequences as well. What will they have to face if the rules are not obeyed? What always works is the involvement of a given person in the process development. Once they participate, they feel the ownership and what follows is their compliance.

If you ignore passive-aggressive behavior, it only gets worse. The carriers of this behavior are very difficult people! Remember that every communication style becomes effective if applied to the right people at the right moment. The same works with the passive-aggressive.

Never lose your alertness; they will test your assertive limits. Handle their manipulations and your life will be considerably calmer.

Be alert for passive-aggressive behavior in your relationships at work and home. Notice how damaging it is. Look for ways you could improve your approach, your communication.

Is there someone in your life who fits this category? Begin to communicate more assertive and efficiently with them. Let them know you are aware of their behavior; it will only help you in long run.

Chapter 14: What's The Difference Between A Psychopath And A Sociopath

Within society, the terms psychopath and sociopath are often used interchangeably. The truth of the matter, however, is that these two terms are very different from one another. Both of them are used to describe someone who has a personality disorder related to the way that they interact with other people and the way that they are able to process different types of emotions, actions and thoughts. Understanding the difference can allow you to better understand the psychopaths (or sociopaths) that you may experience in your life.

Now, there are reasons that these words are used so interchangeably by a number of people in the world. The main reason for this is there are many similarities between these two different types of people. For example, both psychopaths and sociopaths have a tendency to disregard laws, social mores and the rights of others. They both have a tendency to not feel guilt or remorse for their actions and they definitely have a tendency towards violent behavior that is often unexpected and entirely unwarranted. At the same time, these two different types of people will have different traits as well.

A sociopath is less capable of blending in with society. The reason for this is that they are extremely volatile. They may erupt at any time and without any warning at all. They also have trouble staying around other people and hiding their feelings (generally of anger) or experiencing any positive emotions. They find it extremely difficult to interact with others and, as a result, they get nervous, angry and anxious when forced to be around regular people frequently. Because of this, they tend to spend a lot of their time outside of social groups, staying away from other people. They may have a few friends but these are generally complex relationships that are not easily explained or understood.

For a sociopath, being outside of the group and being on their own is not strange. They often find they have little in common truly with other people and have difficulty fitting in even if they do want to (which they generally don't have a reason to). If they do commit a crime it's almost guaranteed to be disorganized and spontaneous. Sociopaths will rarely think out their crimes before they commit them. Generally the feelings and experiences will simply overwhelm them and they will react without thinking.

Now, on the other hand, a psychopath is an extreme planner. They want to have absolute control over everything that they do and, as a result, they carefully plan the exact details of what they are going to do before it happens. They are generally going to have a backup plan and possibly a second backup plan in case something goes wrong. If their plans fail however it can cause them immense distress. This is true of everything that they do as they exercise complete control at all times. This could be over the situations that they find themselves in, their families and especially themselves.

A psychopath will be extremely good at forming emotional attachments and gaining trust because they can easily manipulate the people around them. They actually have excellent abilities to relate to others, hold down a job, and have long-term relationships and more. Because they are extremely calm and collected they often can carry off different types of crimes. They enjoy being completely in control and taking over someone else's life because it gives them a sense of power. Whether they already experience power in their lives is of no consequence.

So what are the main differences? The first is the cause of each. A psychopath is believed to be born. That means they are genetically predisposed toward this type of psychosis and nothing that is done around them is capable of changing that genetic predisposition. They have an underdeveloped portion of their brain that is in charge of controlling their impulses and emotions. This is not to say that someone born with a genetic predisposition will automatically become a psychopath. There are plenty of other factors that will play an important role in this process. If other factors do not align the person will never develop into a full-fledged psychopath. They may develop some of the minor tendencies as discussed above, but they will never advance into hurting others.

On the other hand, a sociopath is someone that is 'created.' This means that they generally undergo some type of trauma during their childhood, which turns them into a sociopath. They are capable of developing emotions and experiencing them but generally push these emotions aside because of the trauma they have faced. They may show some emotions but not others or show those emotions to certain individuals but not others. It's difficult to know when these individuals will be able to interact normally and when they will have a break with reality or the situation at hand.

A psychopath is extremely methodical and will carefully plan out everything that they are going to do while a sociopath is extremely disorganized and incapable of planning things. A sociopath will also experience difficulty in forming relationships or fitting into groups while a psychopath will experience no such problems, capable of fitting easily into any situation. Finally, psychopaths are very good at hiding their tendencies or thoughts that could be considered dark while a sociopath will have more difficulty appearing 'normal.'

Because psychopaths have underdeveloped genes for impulse and emotion they are actually even more dangerous. This is because they do not develop emotional relationships with others nor do they understand these types of relationships. Without these developments they are incapable of caring about their victims as people and see them as dispensable and easy to not only use, but then discard just as quickly. A sociopath, on the other hand, may not relate to the individual that they hurt but they understand the emotions that should go along with these types of behavior. They are more likely to feel remorse after committing an evil act while psychopaths will think only of their own wants and needs.

Conclusion

Sociopaths and psychopaths are considered to be the worst types of humans as they are cold, calculating and can be extremely dangerous. However, as this book shows, they are not always dangerous; many live normal looking lives, carefully controlling their actions and reactions to effectively, hide in plain sight. In fact, it has even been suggested that there are a large number of sociopaths enlisted in the army. Their personalities can be well suited to army life; despite being excellent at manipulating people they are able to take orders from superiors. Of course, respect for their superior is important as is a plan to rise through the ranks and control or manipulate their own team. Their ability to complete tasks such as killing without feeling any guilt or remorse can turn a sociopath into an expert sniper.

Obviously proving that enlisted men and women are sociopaths is not easy, all soldiers are expected to kill and deal with their after effects without cracking up. As sociopaths will generally not draw attention to themselves it is unlikely that the army will highlight an issue, providing they do their job properly. It is not even necessary to prove it; there is plenty of research which suggests there are a number of roles in which you can excel as a sociopath. Political and business leaders often display the characteristics of a sociopath as do soldiers and even, to an extent, some surgeons. In reality the sociopath may actually be a needed member of society!

It is even possible that the increased use of social media is desensitising people to the nastier side of people's characters. In the past if you were obsessed with yourself and your own goals you were, at the very least, a narcissist. It was even possible that you were a sociopath. However, social media revolves around the image of self, you post things simply to get other people's attention and to obtain more followers; this can translate into power. In fact, social media provides the opportunity to influence and manipulate hundreds, if not thousands of people, in one go. It can provide a stage from which to appear charming while misdirecting and manipulating everyone to achieve your own goals. Social media has almost been designed to assist the sociopath indulge their favourite pastime! The most worrying part of this is that behaving in this manner is acceptable and even encouraged on social media.

This type of thinking may not help those who are trapped in a relationship with a sociopath although it may provide them with the opportunity to redirect the sociopath's attention.

This book has been designed to highlight the characteristics of a sociopath and to help you understand what a sociopath is and how this differs from a psychopath; even thought the two words are often taken to mean the same thing. Both disorders come under the heading of antisocial personality disorder, which is one of the recognised personality disorders. You should also have developed an understanding of the common traits which sociopaths display and know how to spot a sociopath. This will give you the option of avoiding them completely, or, if this is not an option, you should now be well equipped to deal with them and even live with them, if necessary.

The brief section on living as a sociopath and the detail on possible treatments and future prospects for those with sociopathy, was designed to broaden your awareness of the disorder. This should help you to understand those who are suffering from this condition and do what you can to help them.

Diagnosing someone with sociopathy is something that must be done by a professional and involves intensive question along with a psychological profile and a complete history. However it is highly unusual for a sociopath to voluntarily submit themselves for a diagnosis. Instead, if you are concerned that someone you know is a sociopath then it is possible to answer sixteen questions online; the result will give you a good idea of whether your friend or relative is a sociopath. You could suggest that they take the test, but if they are a true sociopath they will have no interest in the test or the results; unless they can see it as a useful way to manipulate others in the future.

Research suggests that sociopaths are a product of their environment, with a defect in their neurological patterns. Even if this is the case by the time the sociopath emerges it is too late to reverse the process and it cannot be diagnosed at birth as they have not yet developed into a sociopath. It is possible certain brain patterns can give away the likelihood of a sociopathic personality developing but, at best, this will allow you to attempt to nurture them in such a way that it does not fully develop. In reality this may be extremely difficult. At present this means that there is no known way of preventing or treating a sociopath. As the sociopath matures they will become aware of their ability to manipulate others and that they can undertake a variety of tasks without fear of the consequences.

Understanding the sociopath, their behaviour patterns and how to deal with them will allow you to stay in control of your own life and affairs even if confronted with a sociopath. It will also allow you to help someone suffering from this disorder, if they are open to being helped. The most important thing to remember when dealing with a sociopath is that they have no regret and no guilt; they are incredibly good at manipulating others and calculating the best path for them to get what they want. You are unlikely to be able to out manoeuvre them, or outwit them; it is best to either stay clear or being direct; let them know from the outset that they cannot deter you from your chosen path and always make your decisions before you tell them what you are doing. This will deprive them of the power they are used to and will either mean they leave you to find easier targets or that they accept and respect you. In this way you may be able to spare others from their attention; you may even be able to help keep them from manipulating others. Remain strong no matter what you are faced with!